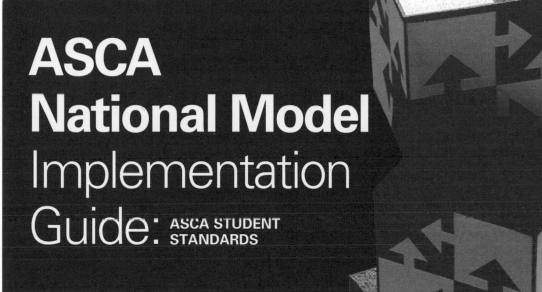

ASCA National Model
Implementation
Guide: ASCA STUDENT STANDARDS

An ASCA National Model® Publication

AMERICAN
SCHOOL
COUNSELOR
ASSOCIATION

1101 King St., Suite 310, Alexandria, VA 22314
(703) 683-ASCA, (800) 306-4722, fax: (703) 997-7572
www.schoolcounselor.org

ISBN 978-1-929289-70-7

Download blank templates and exemplary completed templates from *www.schoolcounselor.org/templates*.

Table of Contents

CHAPTER 1

Understanding the ASCA Student Standards

The 36 ASCA Student Standards: Mindsets & Behaviors for Student Success are broad standards that identify and describe the knowledge, attitudes and skills students should be able to demonstrate as a result of a school counseling program. School counselors use the standards to assess student growth and development, create culturally sustaining strategies and activities and build a program that helps students achieve their highest potential. The ASCA Student Standards can be aligned with the initiatives at the district, state and national levels to reflect local priorities.

To operationalize the standards, school counselors write or select measurable learning objectives that align with specific mindsets or behaviors, which become the foundation for classroom instruction, appraisal and advisement, and counseling activities addressing student developmental needs. The learning objectives directly reflect the school counseling program's vision, mission and goals, as well as the school's academic mission.

Research-Based Standards

The ASCA Student Standards are based on a review of research and college-, career- and life-readiness documents that identify strategies influencing student achievement and academic performance. The ASCA Student Standards are organized on a framework of noncognitive factors presented in the critical literature review "Teaching Adolescents to Become Learners" conducted by the University of Chicago Consortium on Chicago School Research (Farrington et al., 2012).

This literature review recognizes that content knowledge and academic skills are only part of the equation for student success. "School performance is a complex phenomenon, shaped by a wide variety of factors intrinsic to students and the external environment" (Farrington et al., 2012, p. 2). The ASCA Student Standards are based on the evidence of the importance of these factors.

All 36 standards can be applied to any of the three school counseling domains of academic, career and social/emotional development. The school counselor selects a domain and standard based on the needs of the school, classroom, small group or individual.

The standards are arranged within general categories of noncognitive factors related to academic performance as identified in the University of Chicago 2012 literature review. These categories synthesize the "vast array of research literature" (Farrington et al., 2012, p. 8) on noncognitive factors including mindsets, learning strategies, self-management skills and social skills for success.

Category 1: Mindset Standards – Includes standards related to the psycho-social attitudes or beliefs students have about themselves in relation to academic work. These make up the students' belief system as exhibited in behaviors.

Category 2: Behavior Standards – These standards include behaviors commonly associated with being a successful student. These behaviors are visible, outward signs that a student is engaged and putting forth effort to learn. The behaviors are grouped into three subcategories.
- **Learning Strategies:** Processes and tactics students employ to aid in the cognitive work of thinking, remembering or learning.
- **Self-Management Skills:** Continued focus on a goal despite obstacles and avoidance of distractions or temptations to prioritize higher pursuits over lower pleasures.
- **Social Skills:** Acceptable behaviors that improve social interactions, such as those between peers or between students and adults.

Grade-Level Learning Objectives
Grade-level learning objectives are specific, measurable expectations that students attain as they make progress toward the standards. Just as the school counseling program's vision, mission and annual student outcome goals are aligned with the school's academic mission, the school counseling standards and learning objectives also are aligned with academic content standards at the school and district level.

Domains
The ASCA Student Standards can be applied to three broad domains: academic, career and social/emotional development. These domains promote mindsets and behaviors that enhance the learning process and create a culture of college-, career- and life-readiness for every student.

- **Academic Development** – Standards guiding school counseling programs to implement strategies and activities to support and maximize each student's ability to learn.
- **Career Development** – Standards guiding school counseling programs to help students 1) understand the connection between school and the world of work and 2) plan for and make a successful transition from school to postsecondary education and/or the world of work and from job to job across the life span.
- **Social/Emotional Development** – Standards guiding school counseling programs to help students manage emotions and learn and apply interpersonal skills.

WHY STANDARDS?

Student standards have been an integral part of education, often defined and mandated through legislation, such as the Elementary and Secondary Education Act (1965), Improving America's Schools Act (1994), No Child Left Behind (2001), Every Student Succeeds Act (2015). Every subject and grade level in the school building is guided by a set of student standards. Student standards establish the expected student outcomes, defined by changes in student attitudes, knowledge and skills; focus the delivery of instruction to support those attitudes, knowledge and skills; and determine the schema for measuring students' acquisition of the attitudes, knowledge and skills.

The ASCA National Model establishes the ASCA Student Standards, first published in 2014, as the guiding principles for school counselors' work. These 36 standards provide a research-based foundation on which school counselors build programs and deliver activities and services that intentionally target what students need to be effective learners. The standards are the frame for determining content and assessment of the school counselor's delivery of direct and indirect student services.

The purpose of this text is to help school counselors construct the school counseling program and develop direct and indirect student services around those 36 student standards. The ASCA Student Standards are grounded in research, ensuring that school counselors deliver evidence-based content to provide a positive impact on student outcomes. This work raises the credibility and professionalism of the school counseling program. Assessments based on the standards provide the link to how the acquired standards affect student outcomes in achievement, attendance and discipline.

The benefits of operating from a standards paradigm include:
- Standards guide planning, implementation and assessment of the school counseling program.
- Standards reinforce the school counselor's roles and responsibilities. They identify goals that are specifically relevant to school counselors' professional training, skills and credentials.
- Standards enable school counselors to authenticate what belongs in the school counseling program. The standards become the rubric that informs school counselors' choices about what programs and activities are included.
- Standards enable school counselors to validate what does not belong in the school counseling program. Instructional content is streamlined, as only content relating to a standard is a priority.
- Standards ensure continuity of content across settings. The specific design and emphasis of a school counseling program may vary based on student needs, but the scaffolding remains constant.
- Standards anticipate the mobility of students and mediate potential impact. When all school counseling programs operate from the same frame, transitions between schools are eased. Parents, students and all stakeholders know what to expect from the school counseling program. Although the specifics of the program will differ, stakeholders can know that the work will be evidence-based with the ultimate intent to create better outcomes for students.

The ASCA Student Standards link the work of the school counselor with specific student outcomes. School counselors must be guided by the ASCA Student Standards. All school counseling program events, activities, interventions, instruction, appraisal & advisement, counseling, collaborating and consulting should be focused through the lens of the 36 standards. As school counselors determine what to deliver to students, they should reference and connect to the ASCA Student Standards.

In general, school counselors follow a process that begins by identifying a standard for each lesson or activity to be delivered to students. For classroom instruction, one standard is attached to one lesson. A unit of classroom instruction, involving three or more lessons, may have two standards. Small-group instruction and counseling, including four or more sessions, may have one to three standards for the entire group experience. The standard then drives the primary content of the lesson or unit.

Each standard is operationalized via two or more student learning objectives and assessed via pre-/post-assessments. Do not try to address too many standards, as the content becomes diffused and the link to standards is weakened.

In short, the process includes:
1. Identify the ASCA Student Standard.
2. Operationalize the standard.
3. Create the pre-/post-test.
4. Select or develop the lesson/session content.

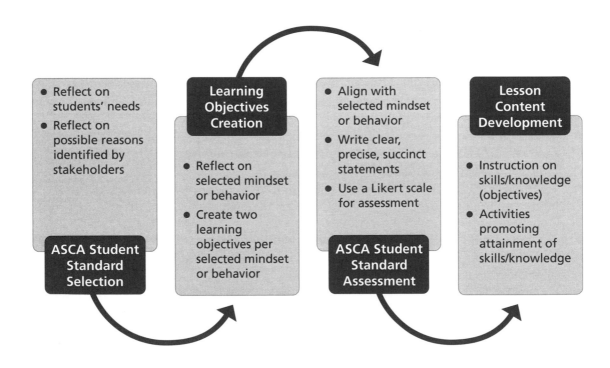

The ASCA National Model guides school counselors in assessing selected direct delivery interventions more intentionally. The process includes:

1. Identify need
2. Collect supplemental data
3. Select ASCA Student Standard
4. Write learning objectives
5. Create pre-/post-assessment
6. Select or develop strategies
7. Administer pre-test
8. Deliver strategies
9. Administer post-test
10. Reflect on areas for improvement

Identify need: School counselors identify a specific student learning challenge revealed in the school's student outcomes (achievement, attendance, discipline). Challenges are revealed when individuals or subsets of students are found to be (a) underperforming in achievement (standardized test scores, grades, credits earned), (b) exhibiting higher absenteeism (absences, late arrivals, early departures, chronically absent) or (c) overrepresented in discipline (offense categories, consequences)

Specific developmental stages or differences may also serve as the basis for school counselor interventions. For example,

- By age 8, children refine their interpersonal relationship skills. Elementary school counselors may routinely deliver classroom instruction on how to make and keep friends, focused through B-SS 2. (Positive, respectful and supportive relationships with students who are similar to and different from them) for all students in third grade.
- Adolescence is a time of physical, emotional and cognitive change. Intense and unpredictable emotions are common. Middle school counselors may focus on B-SMS 7. (Effective coping skills) as a consistent component of their class instruction to help their students manage strong emotions.
- As they continue to move toward increased independence, teens often rely on peers for direction and support. High school counselors may return to B-SS 2. (Positive, respectful and supportive relationships with students who are similar to and different from them) to deliver instruction focused on how to choose friends who will be the most positive and supportive.

If the issue is related to underlying systemic issues, the school counselor advocates to change policies, guidelines and practices to address the systemic issues.

- **Policy issue example:** Students are being suspended for too many absences or three tardies counting as an absence.
- **Strategy:** Talk with administrators about the impact of the procedure, supporting the conversation with specific, detailed data identifying specific students and impact on grades; offer alternatives for keeping students in the school (provide a generic team time experience for students who arrive late, school counselors offer a goal-setting lesson, etc.)

- **Practice issue example:** One teacher strictly adheres to a personal rule regarding absences. Students must ask the teacher for make-up work/assignments. It is not provided automatically. If the work is not submitted within a week of the absence, the grade is entered as a zero. This is not standard practice and is limited to the one teacher.
- **Strategy:** Talk with the teacher and offer suggestions on how to ensure students gain access to work/assignment missed due to late arrival or absence from class. If that yields no change, attend a grade-level or department meeting and discuss various approaches used by teachers within the grade level/department and how to make procedures more consistent and fairer. If still necessary, talk with administrators about the practice and its impact on both attendance and academics.

Collect supplemental data: Gather opinions, beliefs and insights from stakeholders who are directly involved with students experiencing the identified challenge.

Select ASCA Student Standard: Choose a specific ASCA Student Standard that best aligns with the potential factors suggested in the supplemental data.

Write learning objectives: Operationalize the selected standard by writing relevant student learning objectives. The learning objectives identify the specific knowledge and/or skills students need to attain that stated standard.

Create pre-/post-assessment: Develop an assessment based on the learning objectives and selected standard.

Select or develop strategies: Choose strategies, activities and/or interventions to facilitate attainment of the learning objectives; develop your own if none exist.

Administer pre-test: Use the pre-test to determine targeted students' baseline knowledge and skills.

Deliver strategies: Implement the activity/lesson/group.

Administer post-test: Assess students' acquisition of the learning objectives.

Reflect on areas for improvement: What worked, what didn't and how can you make it better next time?

The 36 ASCA Student Standards for school counseling programs are:

M 1. Belief in development of whole self, including a healthy balance of mental, social/emotional and physical well-being

M 2. Sense of acceptance, respect, support and inclusion for self and others in the school environment

M 3. Positive attitude toward work and learning

M 4. Self-confidence in ability to succeed

M 5. Belief in using abilities to their fullest to achieve high-quality results and outcomes

M 6. Understanding that postsecondary education and lifelong learning are necessary for long-term success

B-LS 1. Critical-thinking skills to make informed decisions

B-LS 2. Creative approach to learning, tasks and problem solving

B-LS 3. Time-management, organizational and study skills

B-LS 4. Self-motivation and self-direction for learning

B-LS 5. Media and technology skills to enhance learning

B-LS 6. High standards of quality for tasks and activities

B-LS 7. Long- and short-term academic, career and social/emotional goals

B-LS 8. Engagement in challenging coursework

B-LS 9. Decision-making informed by gathering evidence, getting others' perspectives and recognizing personal bias

B-LS 10. Participation in enrichment and extracurricular activities

B-SMS 1. Responsibility for self and actions

B-SMS 2. Self-discipline and self-control

B-SMS 3. Independent work

B-SMS 4. Delayed gratification for long-term rewards

B-SMS 5. Perseverance to achieve long- and short-term goals

B-SMS 6. Ability to identify and overcome barriers to learning

B-SMS 7. Effective coping skills

B-SMS 8. Balance of school, home and community activities

B-SMS 9. Personal safety skills

B-SMS 10. Ability to manage transitions and adapt to change

B-SS 1. Effective oral and written communication skills and listening skills

B-SS 2. Positive, respectful and supportive relationships with students who are similar to and different from them

B-SS 3. Positive relationships with adults to support success

B-SS 4. Empathy

B-SS 5. Ethical decision-making and social responsibility

B-SS 6. Effective collaboration and cooperation skills

B-SS 7. Leadership and teamwork skills to work effectively in diverse teams

B-SS 8. Advocacy skills for self and others and ability to assert self, when necessary

B-SS 9. Social maturity and behaviors appropriate to the situation and environment

B-SS 10. Cultural awareness, sensitivity and responsiveness

USING THE ASCA STUDENT STANDARDS

Mindset and behavior standards guide the development and/or selection of program activities.

School counselors are often asked to assume responsibility for a variety of programs and may struggle with determining the appropriateness of a specific activity or may feel pressured to acquiesce. Rather than trying to debate or defend what might appear to be a personal preference, employ the 36 statements as the rubric for making the decision. It moves the discussion from whether the school counselor should accept responsibility to whether the activity or event supports the student standards of the school counseling program.

If the activity does not match the program's standards, then it is not a school counseling program priority.

Mindset and behavior standards provide the basis for school counselor instruction, appraisal & advisement, and counseling.

School counselors have limited time and access for delivery of classroom instruction and small-group experiences. Therefore, those opportunities must be purposeful, strategic and constructive. Well-designed instructional activities delivered based on a specifically targeted standard begin with an assumption of positive impact since it is based on an essential knowledge, attitude or skill, evidenced in research. Groups developed around two or three ASCA Student Standards that are intentionally chosen to match the group members' specific needs have the best chance of positive impact, as they are grounded in research-identified constructs. Establishing the standards as the lens for focusing lessons, activities, instruction and counseling yields better strategies, supported by research, connected to student needs and delivered with intentionality. This happens when school counselors start with a standard and then determine how to best deliver it to students. Consider the adage, "Begin with the end in mind." The standard is your goal for the students; it is the "end." Start with it, then design, adapt or select the lesson/activity that will move the students toward it.

Mindset and behavior standards drive the creation of meaningful assessments of student learning.

Assessments of school counseling activities serve two purposes: 1) to determine if students learned/acquired the intended content and 2) to link the learning/acquisition of delivered content to student outcomes (achievement, attendance, discipline). Since the content of the activity starts with a selected student standard, the assessment also must start there. The selected standard is operationalized by creating specific, relevant student learning objectives. The learning objectives then become the basis of assessment items.

Mindset and behavior standards provide evidence that knowledge, attitudes and skills acquired through school counselor instruction, appraisal & advisement, and counseling affect student outcomes (achievement, attendance, discipline).

The process described in Example 1 occurs before any activity or instruction is provided. With all of this identified at the onset, the content of what should be delivered becomes obvious, and the specifics of how to deliver the content are improved. The assessment (Mindsets & Behaviors data) is delivered before and after the content. If the students show improved scores on the post-assessment, indicating they learned what the school counselor planned and delivered, it is then hoped that students have clarified their futures and, as a result, have improved their classroom performance in advanced classes (outcome data/achievement). The evidence suggests that the intervention of helping students select post-secondary options had a positive impact on their grades (achievement) in advanced classes.

Example 1:

A group of students are performing at minimally acceptable levels in their advanced classes. Based on conversations you have with students, their parents and teachers, you discover:
- Students in the targeted group reveal they have not yet identified any postsecondary options.
- Students also reveal a lack of discernment, knowledge or processes for making decisions about postsecondary options.

You select standard B-LS 1. (Critical-thinking skills to make informed decisions). The selected standard (B-LS 1.) serves as the basis for creating/selecting the student learning objectives, which then drive the content of what will be delivered. You write the following learning objectives:
- Students will select three–five postsecondary options for indepth research.
- Students will identify relevant sources of data for choosing postsecondary options.
- Students will collect and analyze information from data sources.
- Students will apply a problem-solving model based on researched information.

The student learning objectives become the basis for the assessment items. These can be presented using a Likert-scale response.
- I know three possible postsecondary options I am considering.
- I know how to find the pros and cons for selecting a postsecondary option.
- I know how to compare the pros and cons for multiple postsecondary options.
- I can make a reasoned argument for selecting one postsecondary option.

It is also possible to use the same stems above as short-answer questions. Rather than indicating on a Likert scale the degree to which students self-report their capacity, make each a question that can be answered simply. Simplicity is important because you will be scoring each of these.
- Name three possible postsecondary options you are considering.
- What sources might you use to identify the pros and cons for selecting the options named above?
- Describe your thinking on how to evaluate a list of pros and cons.
- Choose one of your postsecondary options currently under consideration and identify three or more reasons why it is the best choice.

Although short-answer questions offer a more authentic revelation of what students know or can do, they do require more time. You might consider a hybrid of Likert scale self-reports and one short answer. The design is up to you. Just remember, whatever you ask, you must score.

Mindset and behavior standards offer ways to evaluate delivery of services.

Returning to Example 1, what if the students' classroom performance in advanced classes does not improve? Because the assessment and intervention are well-defined and targeted, it is easy to analyze what might have happened. You might consider your choice of standards, the ways in which the standard was operationalized through learning objective statements, how it was measured and whether the intervention allowed time for mastery of the standard. All these offer points through which more can be discovered.

- Were those conversations broad enough to include other possibilities? Did I focus too quickly on the postsecondary piece? What else could explain their classroom performance? How can those questions be asked more effectively, or what other questions could be asked to discover more?
- Were there other standards that could have been a better choice? Maybe B-LS 4. (Self-motivation and self-direction to learning) was a closer match to their classroom underperformance.
- Were the objective statements too focused on postsecondary options? What else could I have used for improving their problems-solving skills?
- Were my activities delivered well? Were they quality activities?
- Did the students learn what I hoped? Was there improvement in the pre-/post-scores? If there was improvement, why did it not improve their classroom performance?

All of these represent ways to evaluate the delivery of this single intervention. Mindset and behavior standards serve as the basis for school counselor reflection on the strategy and how to do it better next time.

STUDENT LEARNING OBJECTIVES

The 36 student standards are big ideas. They represent overarching concepts and broad skills. They provide the learning destination but not the path to get there. In fact, most have a variety of ways to be reached. To be truly useful, they must be operationalized. Identifying what students need to believe, know or be able to do helps clear the pathway to realizing the standard.

Learning objectives describe the desired knowledge, attitude and skills of students. These are statements that specify what you believe students need to move toward attainment of the stated standard. They are specific, measurable expectations that students attain as they make progress toward the standards. School counselors may align learning objectives with their state's academic standards. This alignment helps students meet these college- and career-readiness standards in collaboration with academic content taught in core areas in the classroom. It also helps school counselors directly align with academic instruction. Alternately, you can create your own learning objectives based on your professional judgment. To make the mindset and behavior standards most useful, create or think about the specific knowledge, attitudes and skills needed.

A variety of student learning objectives are provided for each of the 30 behavioral student standards. These are provided in these chapters:
- Chapter 3: Learning Strategies, page 33
- Chapter 4: Self-Management Skills, page 57
- Chapter 5: Social Skills, page 81

As you consider the learning objectives in this guide, remember that they don't represent all possibilities. In addition, the statements can be modified. The learning objectives provided offer examples that may be used as they are written, adapted to meet specific developmental needs or used as a model for writing new objectives.

For example, one learning objective identified for B-SS 2 (Positive, respectful and supportive relationships with students who are similar to and different from them) deals with recognizing and interpreting cues: Students will recognize and interpret verbal and nonverbal social cues.

Depending on students' age or developmental level, it may be more appropriate to focus on a subset of this objective. It might be best if the to narrow the focus to one of these possibilities:
- Students will recognize facial cues.
- Students will recognize verbal cues from teachers.
- Students will recognize facial cues that signal anger.

It is also possible to expand a learning objective for those at more advanced levels.
- Students will interpret words and phrases that insinuate hostility or intimidation.

Finally, the learning objective may provide a model for creating a new objective. Perhaps, the focus needs to be grounded in social experiences. The new objective might change the focus away from interpreting cues to recognizing the dynamics within the social exchange.
- Students will recognize and interpret the primary purpose of school interactions between and among students.

Writing Learning Objectives

Learning objective statements describe what students will know, believe or be able to do. Since it is about the student, it should begin with students as the subject of the sentence.

Students will (action verb) (describe knowledge or skill). Following are some suggestions from Bloom's Taxonomy (Shabatura, 2013; Wilson, 2020):
- Remembering: define, describe, list, state, name
- Understanding: classify, compare, contrast, describe, employ, explain, illustrate, interpret
- Applying: construct, determine, develop, employ, predict, solve, teach
- Analyzing: analyze, classify, contrast, correlate, differentiate, explain, illustrate, infer
- Evaluating: appraise, argue, assess, compare, critique, debate, justify, persuade, predict
- Creating: collaborate, compile, compose, construct, create, design, develop, negotiate, produce, revise, solve, write

Writing the statement in active voice adds clarity, activity and measurability. Often, first attempts at writing objectives will include "students will be able to" opening. Converting from passive to active voice simply requires removing the "be able to" words from the statement.

Example: School counselors will be able to write measurable learning objectives.
School counselors will ~~be able to~~ write measurable learning objectives.
School counselors will write measurable learning objectives.

Learning Objective Do's
■ Include a present tense action verb
■ Be clear and concise
■ Include measurable and/or observable terms

Learning Objective Don'ts
■ Include vague words
■ Include specific activity (through a group experience)
■ Write in passive voice

MINDSETS & BEHAVIORS DATA & ASSESSMENTS

The ASCA National Model offers the clearest definitions for assessing school counselors' work based on the ASCA Student Standards. Although these standards provide the foundation for the content and strategies delivered, they also provide the frame for determining if students met the targeted standard. School counselors can quickly and easily assess students' acquisition of the observable knowledge and skills associated with the targeted student standard.

Example: An identified group of students with no documentation of special needs or disabilities earned grades lower than their peers. While collecting the supplemental data, school counselors discover the following:
■ Teachers reported these students are not completing the day-to-day work required, whether at home or in class.
■ Students' parents/guardians offered other ideas, suggesting the students lack interest in the subject matter, the homework was difficult to manage due to lack of resources or student noncompliance, and/or the students were easily frustrated with the assigned tasks and gave up.
■ Conversations with the students indicate they believe the work is too hard, too boring or they just don't get home with what they need from school. Several students also mentioned the classroom is noisy and very little time is provided to begin tasks. By the time they get home, they no longer know what or how to do the task.

This situation offers a variety of possibilities for what is happening with the students. School counselors use their professional knowledge and training to focus on what is believed to be essential. For purposes of this example, the school counselor selects the standard B-SMS 1. (Responsibility for self and action).

To operationalize that standard (B-SMS 1) the school counselor focuses on a single objective: Students will complete all assignments for math class.

With a focus on assignment completion, specific interventions are selected or developed. For this example, the school counselor provided instruction around strategies for remembering assignments and materials along with procedural steps for the task completion. In addition, the school counselor offered opportunities for working on assigned tasks and linked students to resources for math assistance and tutoring. Before and after the interventions were delivered, the school counselor assessed students' self-reports around task completion with the following pre-test:

I finish at least two math problems on an assignment in class.

1. Never   **2. 1-2 times a week**   **3. 3-4 times a week**   **4. Every assignment**

I get all my homework completed on time.

1. Never   **2. 1-2 times a week**   **3. 3-4 times a week**   **4. Every assignment**

I submit my homework when it is due.

1. Never   **2. 1-2 times a week**   **3. 3-4 times a week**   **4. Every assignment**

Comparing students' answers before and after the interventions provides information on students learning to get their math assignments completed. Of course, the additional step for comparing math grades is essential. Based on the post-test data, the school counselor learns if the strategies worked, need adjusting or need to be entirely different.

Comparisons rely on calculating the average student response for each assessment item, a process described in "Making DATA Work."

Calculating Average Student Response on Likert Scale

Identify the number of students who completed the assessment. (50)

For assessment item #1, multiple the number of students who circled/selected each answer choice with the number value of the answer choice.

20 students selected 1. Never	**20 X 1 = 20**
17 students selected 2. Sometimes	**17 X 2 = 34**
6 students selected 3. Often	**6 X 3 = 18**
7 students selected 4. Always	**7 X 4 = 28**

Add the products to get a sum.

20 + 34 + 18 + 28 = 100

Divide the sum by the number of students who completed the assessment.

100 ÷ 50 = 2

The result is the average student response for item #1.

Average student response is 2 (sometimes finish at least 2 problems)

Alignment with ASCA National Model Templates

Several templates from the ASCA National Model include the ASCA Student Standards, learning objectives and assessments. Always check the website, *www.schoolcounselor.org/ templates* for the most current templates and examples. The templates related to the ASCA Student Standards are:

- Annual student outcome goal plan
- Classroom and group instruction results report
- Closing-the-gap action plan
- Lesson plans

Remember:

- Identify one ASCA Student Standard for a lesson, strategy or activity.
- Base the standard selection on the students' specific needs and the lesson's purpose.
- Use the selected student standard to drive the selection or creation of the learning objectives.
- Use the learning objectives to drive the items on the pre-/post-assessment.

CHAPTER 2

Mindset Standards

The six mindsets in the ASCA Student Standards describe the psycho-social attitudes or beliefs students have about themselves in relation to academic work. These standards make up students' belief system. Mindsets are more readily recognized through the behaviors a student demonstrates. They are inferred based on what is observed, making them vulnerable to bias, inaccurate assumptions or misunderstandings. Therefore, the mindset standards do not have correlating learning objectives.

Psychologist Albert Bandura (1977) described self-efficacy as the belief in one's own capacity to do what is necessary to achieve. That foundational work continues to be validated as important to academic achievement. Students' belief about their ability to produce a desired goal affects whether they attempt goal setting, how much work they are willing to do toward that goal and how long they will work for the goal. Their belief in their own personal ability to learn content or to perform academic tasks affects their motivation and effort.

Additionally, attribution theory affirms that individuals who attribute failures to personal ability tend to withhold effort in future tasks. Without these mindsets, students may struggle to stay engaged, take academic risks, persist through challenges and/or expect a positive outcome for their own academic endeavors.

The book "Teaching Adolescents to Become Learners" (Farrington et al., 2012), one of the key sources for the ASCA Student Standards development, identifies several takeaways:
- Interventions directed at changing students' mindsets can have lasting effects on school performance.
- Psycho-social approaches may have an important impact on closing racial/ethnic gaps in student performance and attainment.
- Students who believe they have a meaningful place in the class or school are more likely to engage in positive academic behaviors, believe themselves to be more competent and have a stronger sense of identity.
- Students who believe that personal effort can positively affect their academic outcomes are more likely to be motivated and persistent in their academic behaviors.

- What students believe about their own intelligence or competence is a better predictor of school performance than their measured ability.
- When students feel confident, they are more likely to engage in the academic work. Basically, if they think they can, they try harder.
- Students' choices, persistence and performance at academic tasks is strongly influenced by how much value they ascribe to the task. If they find a task interesting or relevant to their future goals/aspirations, they will work harder.

School counselors' work encourages students to hold these beliefs, not through direct instruction but in the context of how school counselors interact with and nurture their students. Serving as a constant advocate and coach, school counselors create environments, systems and opportunities for these six foundational beliefs in all students.

The mindsets are inferred from observable student behaviors, often described in the learning objectives, which operationalize the behavioral student standards of learning strategies, self-management skills and social skills. Therefore, the behavioral standards all include the identification of "foundational mindsets" – those that support the stated standard and its corresponding learning objectives. It may be helpful to hold those specified student mindsets as background for providing instruction around those learning objectives.

ASCA STUDENT STANDARDS: MINDSETS

M 1. Belief in development of whole self, including a healthy balance of mental, social/emotional, and physical well-being

The M 1. standard reflects the students' engagement, commitment and lifestyle, including presence or absence of healthy habits. It also encompasses students' commitment level. Those who hold this stated belief participate at higher levels.

Effective strategies to use or suggest to teachers might include:
- Provide direct instruction on healthy habits, including nutrition, exercise and sleep/rest. Many students, and their parents, hold faulty beliefs around the basic health requirements for specific age groups.
- Provide direct instruction on mindfulness. Define it and provide strategies commonly associated strategies.
- Encourage teachers to embed "mindful moments" during and between classes.
- Consider schoolwide practices that include mindfulness activities. For example, include a simple mindful exercise in morning announcements/broadcasts.
- Develop a culture of a growth mindset, including students, faculty/staff and parents/guardians in the instruction, planning and practice.
- Adopt a schoolwide social/emotional learning curriculum. Consider programs using classroom teachers as the instructors. This expands the amount of time devoted to SEL and builds a larger consortium of those with knowledge and practice.
- Examine the visuals of the school building and consider if and how much they contribute to the development of the whole self. Identify what might be missing, outdated or inaccurate, and replace them with more appropriate displays.

- Establish a working committee dedicated to the development, implementation and maintenance of specific programs, clubs and practices focused on students' mental, social/emotional and physical health.

M 2. Sense of acceptance, respect, support and inclusion for self and others in the school environment

Students need a sense of belonging in the school environment, feeling wanted, valued and respected by both peers and adults. Believing that one has a meaningful contribution to make to the class or school enables students to fully participate, becoming fully engaged in school life, including school activities and clubs (Farrington et al., 2012, p. 30).

Students' sense of belonging starts with teachers. Teachers must be intentional about building community in their classrooms as well as working to connect with individual students. Teachers may also be unaware of what might be limiting a student's sense of belonging. All of this can be overwhelming for teachers, who already have far too much to do. They need support and instruction on how to accomplish this. School counselors can provide the necessary support and instruction.

Effective strategies to use or suggest to teachers might include:
- Build community in a classroom
  - Show interest in all students. Highlight each student in positive ways by naming specific contributions students make to the class, discussions or work; talking positively about each student in public settings; and creating opportunities for students to share their personal talents/skills/accomplishments.
  - Establish a schedule for periodic student presentations on personal interests/talents/circumstances/experiences – anything that fosters communication about themselves and strengthens student identity.
  - Always leave one desk empty. Whenever a new student arrives, the desk is there and available, ensuring additions are welcomed rather than simply accommodated.
  - Establish clear procedures for assigning groups and partner work. Teachers must create in-class student groupings and partnerships with careful thought and reflection and ensure respectful, kind practices when student choice is offered for forming those groupings.
  - Foster peer relationships and provide time and space for those relationships to grow.
  - Have a well-managed classroom with specific procedures and routines.
  - Ask students what they need/want and then discuss if/how it can be incorporated into the classroom.
- Pay attention to students who are missing class or school. It can be an indicator that the student is not experiencing that sense of belonging.
- Poll students (allow anonymity) to discover how they are feeling about school belongingness and to identify the reasons they report for not feeling as though they belong.
- Learn and use students' names. Greet them when they arrive.
- Create a culture of respectful language and words. Also, consider the use of pronouns, preferred names, microaggressions and how to confront and eliminate these. Finally, review and remove traditional practices, such as dividing into teams by boys/girls.
- Create a display that acknowledges and celebrates all students and their family heritage/culture.

- Review student membership in various courses, clubs and activities and consider how that membership reflects the overall student population. Look at various publications and identify who is and is not included in recognitions and membership.
- Continue to ask who is not being successful in the school. It can be easy to get focused on those who are achieving and excelling, especially when that represents most of the student population. In schools identified as "high-achieving," it is important to identify any/all students who are not meeting that standard. There is always work to be done and students who need their school counselor to stand for them until all standards of success are operating at 100% for all students.

M 3. Positive attitude toward work and learning

Students with a positive attitude toward work and learning demonstrate a personal value for learning course content. They tolerate mistakes and take academic risks. When students have a positive attitude, when they believe they will be successful, they work harder and sustain the effort. When they feel confident, students engage. This positive attitude then contributes to improved academic outcomes.

Effective strategies to use or suggest to teachers might include:
- Foster an environment focused on growth mindsets for all.
- Celebrate diversity.
- Implement current best practice for fostering student motivation.
- Limit extrinsic motivation systems to only those few students who may need an extra incentive. Fade out the extrinsic rewards as quickly as possible.
- Challenge students' word use. For example, emphasize the power of "yet." Change "I can't do this" to "I can't do this yet."
- Ask students to create a personal list of reasons for striving in school. Identify why school is important. Articulate desired life goals along with a statement of what makes those goals important. Define what might happen if they do not work hard.
- Help students explore their reasons for any negative or less-than-positive feelings about school. Determine which reasons might be redirected, reframed or changed, and focus on those. Create a plan for what to do.
- Use cognitive behavioral therapy techniques. Identify students' thought processes and how these might be affecting their attitude toward school.
- Review the list of irrational thoughts with students. Discuss which of these might be affecting students' feelings and how to correct the faulty thinking.
- Help students identify what makes them happy. Help them describe, in detail, the places, people, things that generate feelings of contentment, happiness or excitement. Help them use these images/thoughts to elicit those positive feelings when they begin to feel overwhelmed, helpless or hopeless in school.
- Work with students to reflect on the positives of the school experience. Keeping a journal of positives can help change the focus on their daily thoughts and interrupt any negativity.
- Teach students about the powerful influence those around us have on our thoughts, feelings and moods. Help students identify the friends who are encouraging them vs. those who are bringing negativity. Explore ways to counter the negativity and when it might be best to adjust friendship circles.

- Help students identify positive, diverse people with whom to associate. Reinforce the benefits.
- Help students reflect on what they have learned and can learn rather than the final grades. Grades can feel overwhelming or too far in the future to provide motivation for today. Instead, think about what can be or was learned today.
- Help students identify personal negative self-talk. Teach them thought-stopping techniques. Work with them to create affirmations to replace the negative thoughts.
- Employ the strategies of solution-focused counseling (looking for exceptions, scaling, miracle question and trusting in the students' capacity).

M 4. Self-confidence in ability to succeed

Students' beliefs about their own intelligence are a critical factor that affects not only their learning, self-control and persistence but also the quality of their relationships with peers and adults (Farrington et al., 2012, p. 6).

Attribution error theory asserts that how individuals assign reasons for successes and failures affects and reveals personal beliefs about their capabilities. When successes are over-assigned to external reasons (something was easy or the teacher was being generous in the assessment), the individual minimizes or underrates personal capacity. Failures attributed to internal reasons (lack of intelligence, poor memory skills, being a poor student) strengthen the negative self-perceptions and limit the individual's will to try. These errors in thinking must be discovered and countered.

Effective strategies to use or suggest to teachers might include:
- Teach, promote growth mindsets.
- Teach attribution theory to students, faculty/staff and parents/guardians.
- Employ narrative techniques that story and re-story personal events of failure and success.
- Incorporate solution-focused techniques in counseling sessions.
- Add an "On-A-Roll" program that recognizes students who have demonstrated improvement in a class or grade. This could operate in conjunction with typical honor roll programs.
- Understand the difference between praise and encouragement.
- Teach adults who are interacting with students the difference between praise and encouragement.
- Include a variety of student interest groups, clubs and activities that facilitate recognition of a variety of talents, skills and contributions of students.
- Deliver explicit instruction on the value of mistakes.
- Use literature featuring individuals who overcome barriers, self-doubts, lack of resources, etc. to achieve a personal goal. As you are selecting stories and books, include representation from all cultures. In addition, find those that feature smaller goals. For example, while you can include someone who makes it to the Olympics and earns a gold medal, balance this with stories that have important but less-public achievements.
- Build a culture of goal setting and goal work in the school. There is growing evidence of increased positive academic outcomes in classrooms that spend weekly time on goal work with students.

M 5. Belief in using abilities to their fullest to achieve high-quality results and outcomes

The belief in using one's abilities to achieve is reflected in students' course selections, persistence, perseverance and time devoted to tasks required to be successful.

The University of Chicago study indicated that students choose, persist and perform academic tasks based on how much value they ascribe to each task. If the task is seen as interesting or important to their future aspirations, they will work harder.

Courses with a reputation for being fun and interesting tend to have students enroll in them. Creative teaching strategies and positive student/teacher relationships make learning fun. The University of Chicago study affirms that interesting coursework or course tasks tend to engender students working at a higher level.

Connecting coursework, especially more rigorous coursework, to specific career possibilities increases the likelihood students will consider enrolling. For example, students might be more likely to enroll in an AP class in art and design if they understand how it might contribute to acceptance into an engineering school and a possible architectural career. Likewise, specific tasks within courses can be linked to future aspirations. Linking tasks and coursework to the future increases the perceived value, giving students specific reasons to work for it.

Finally, jobs in the future are more likely to require some postsecondary education/training. A report by the U.S. Bureau of Labor Statistics (2019) predicted job increases in health care and clean energy, fields which tend to require more education/training, and declining manufacturing jobs, which have a greater number of positions that require only a high school diploma. Furthermore, that report stated the number of jobs requiring masters' degrees will grow three times faster than those requiring high school only. It is increasingly important for students to situate themselves to be eligible for those postsecondary options. We must be explicit and honest in connecting rigorous coursework and improved academic outcomes to improved life outcomes.

Effective strategies to use or suggest to teachers might include:
- Focus on goal work with students (includes identifying the goal and writing it clearly, developing a specific plan to achieve the goal, monitoring one's own progress toward the goal, celebrating intermittent and ultimate successes and creating new goals).
- Provide instruction on identifying and establishing educational priorities for life success.
- Help students identify links between actions and outcomes. Connect academic performance to enhanced postsecondary options and, ultimately, career possibilities.
- Help students navigate any barriers that may limit their recognition and use of their own abilities. Challenge policies and procedures that might limit access to rigor. Engage in professional development supporting enhanced classroom environments. Participate in regular conversations with administrators about any concerns that become evident regarding all students' progress toward high-quality results and outcomes.
- Create student leadership opportunities/programs (peer mediation, peer leadership, peer tutoring, student ambassadors, near-peer mentoring).
- Develop varied recognition strategies for celebrating all skills/talents/interests (beyond honor roll).

- Develop and promote varied skill- interest-based programs and activities facilitating student growth in a variety of areas (athletics, arts, honors programs, etc.).
- Incorporate independent-learning projects. Giving students some choice over what and how a project can be completed is connected to higher-level work by the student.
- Market or promote the optional rigorous courses to increase student participation. Consider linking specific courses to potential future benefits for students (e.g., a student interested in architecture may enroll in an advanced drawing class).
- Be a role model for fun, creative teaching/learning experiences.

M 6. Understanding that postsecondary education and lifelong learning are necessary for long-term career success.

Identifying desired life outcomes, such as lifestyles, vocations and environments, increases a student's understanding of how the present affects future aspirations. This helps students create clear long-term goals and develop plans for achieving them. In addition, they can link today's learning and tasks to those future goals. School counselors work directly on all students' college and career readiness. That work is extended as school counselors share their expertise with others in the school.

Effective strategies to use or suggest to teachers might include:
- Focus on goal work (includes identifying goal and writing it clearly, developing a specific plan to achieve the goal, monitoring one's own progress toward the goal, celebrating intermittent and ultimate successes, and creating new goals).
- Provide instruction on postsecondary opportunities. Focus on a variety of options, the requirements and benefits of each, and how/if each links to students' future life goals/plans.
- Provide instruction on career exploration and planning. Focus on linking interests and skills to career options and the requirements associated with each. Be sure to address a variety of jobs within any category. Do not limit choices to the popular or generally esteemed job within the field; rather, include jobs at a variety of levels. For example, include more than physician when discussing the medical field. Include med techs, nurses and nursing assistance, specialized groups, etc.
- Include information on required continuing professional development for jobs.
- Provide instruction on and facilitate exploration of lifestyles and associated requirements to realize desired futures. Have students identify where and how they might want to live as a young adult. Work backward to determine how much that lifestyle and location might cost in terms of education, workload and finances, and then research what kinds of jobs in their preferred career cluster might match those requirements.
- Create a culture of promoting a variety of postsecondary experiences. Discuss the benefits/costs of traditional college/university, specialty training, trade school, apprenticeships, military service and immediate job entry. Discuss nontraditional paths for obtaining postsecondary education.
- Talk about career salaries in terms of range rather than averages. The range of salaries is more authentic and honest in depicting the potential payoffs of a specific career.
- Implement programs allowing students to experience the world of work: job shadowing, internships, career fairs, classroom guests, etc. Be sure these programs are accessible for all students. Develop specific supports that help students circumvent any barriers for participation.

- Build an inventory of resources for pursuing postsecondary options and facilitate access to those resources for all students.

CONNECTING BEHAVIOR STANDARDS WITH THE SIX MINDSETS

School counselors foster students' mindsets, not through direct instruction but through interactions acknowledging students' experiences and nurturing their potential. The mindsets provide the foundations, which enables the desired behaviors.

The chart below demonstrates which mindsets may be connected to each of the behavior standards. The connections are not rigid or fixed; they vary with individuals and their circumstances. In addition, remember that mindsets may only be inferred. They are viewed through one's own personal filters and vulnerable to our own assumptions and biases.

As school counselors, we work to facilitate student acquisition of the behavior standards. An exploration of the absence or presence of the mindsets within the students supports that work. Ask questions of students that might reveal their mindsets. Challenge those that are counter to the positive development of the behavior standard. Restate and reframe students' personal reflections toward more positive beliefs. Use the mindset standards to support the acquisition of the behavior standards.

Behavior Standards Connected to Mindset Standards

	Behavior Standard	Mindset Standards
B-LS 1.	Critical-thinking skills to make informed decisions	M 1. Belief in development of whole self, including a healthy balance of mental, social/emotional, and physical well-being M 2. Self-confidence in ability to succeed M 4. Understanding that postsecondary education and lifelong learning are necessary for long-term career success
B-LS 2.	Creative approach to learning, tasks and problem solving	M 1. Belief in development of whole self, including a healthy balance of mental, social/emotional, and physical well-being M 4. Self-confidence in ability to succeed M 5. Belief in using abilities to their fullest to achieve high-quality results and outcomes
B-LS 3.	Time-management, organizational and study skills	M 3. Positive attitude toward work and learning M 5. Belief in using abilities to their fullest to achieve high-quality results and outcomes M 6. Understanding that postsecondary education and lifelong learning are necessary for long-term career success

	Behavior Standard	Mindset Standards
B-LS 4.	Self-motivation and self- direction for learning	M 3. Positive attitude toward work and learning M 4. Self-confidence in ability to succeed M 5. Belief in using abilities to their fullest to achieve high-quality results and outcomes M 6. Understanding that postsecondary education and lifelong learning are necessary for long-term career success
B-LS 5.	Media and technology skills to enhance learning	M 5. Belief in using abilities to their fullest to achieve high-quality results and outcomes M 6. Understanding that postsecondary education and lifelong learning are necessary for long-term career success
B-LS 6.	High-quality standards for tasks and activities	M 1. Belief in development of whole self, including a healthy balance of mental, social/emotional, and physical well-being M 3. Positive attitude toward work and learning M 5. Belief in using abilities to their fullest to achieve high-quality results and outcomes M 6. Understanding that postsecondary education and lifelong learning are necessary for long-term career success
B-LS 7.	Long- and short-term academic, career and social/ emotional goals	M 1. Belief in development of whole self, including a healthy balance of mental, social/emotional, and physical well-being M 2. Self-confidence in ability to succeed M 4. Understanding that postsecondary education and lifelong learning are necessary for long-term career success M 5. Belief in using abilities to their fullest to achieve high-quality results and outcomes
B-LS 8.	Long- and short-term academic, career and social/ emotional goals	M 3. Positive attitude toward work and learning M 4. Self-confidence in ability to succeed M 5. Belief in using abilities to their fullest to achieve high-quality results and outcomes M 6. Understanding that postsecondary education and lifelong learning are necessary for long-term career success

	Behavior Standard	Mindset Standards
B-LS 9.	Decision-making informed by gathering evidence, getting others' perspectives and recognizing personal bias	M 5. Belief in using abilities to their fullest to achieve high-quality results and outcomes M 6. Understanding that postsecondary education and lifelong learning are necessary for long-term career success
B-LS 10.	Participation in enrichment and extracurricular activities	M 1. Belief in development of whole self, including a healthy balance of mental, social/emotional, and physical well-being M 2. Sense of acceptance, respect, support and inclusion for self and others in the school environment M 4. Self-confidence in ability to succeed
B-SMS 1.	Responsibility for self and actions	M 4. Self-confidence in ability to succeed M 5. Belief in using abilities to their fullest to achieve high-quality results and outcomes M 6. Understanding that postsecondary education and lifelong learning are necessary for long-term career success
B-SMS 2.	Self-discipline and self-control	M 4. Self-confidence in ability to succeed M 6. Understanding that postsecondary education and lifelong learning are necessary for long-term career success
B-SMS 3.	Independent work	M 3. Positive attitude toward work and learning M 4. Self-confidence in ability to succeed M 5. Belief in using abilities to their fullest to achieve high-quality results and outcomes M 6. Understanding that postsecondary education and lifelong learning are necessary for long-term career success
B-SMS 4.	Delayed gratification for long-term rewards	M 3. Positive attitude toward work and learning M 5. Belief in using abilities to their fullest to achieve high-quality results and outcomes M 6. Understanding that postsecondary education and lifelong learning are necessary for long-term career success

	Behavior Standard	Mindset Standards
B-SMS 5.	Perseverance to achieve long- and short-term goals	M 1. Belief in development of whole self, including a healthy balance of mental, social/emotional, and physical well-being M 3. Positive attitude toward work and learning M 5. Belief in using abilities to their fullest to achieve high-quality results and outcomes M 6. Understanding that postsecondary education and lifelong learning are necessary for long-term career success
B-SMS 6.	Ability to identify and overcome barriers	M 3. Positive attitude toward work and learning M 4. Self-confidence in ability to succeed
B-SMS 7.	Effective coping skills	M 3. Positive attitude toward work and learning M 4. Self-confidence in ability to succeed
B-SMS 8.	Balance of school, home and community activities	M 1. Belief in development of whole self, including a healthy balance of mental, social/emotional, and physical well-being M 2. Sense of acceptance, respect, support and inclusion for self and others in the school environment M 5. Belief in using abilities to their fullest to achieve high-quality results and outcomes
B-SMS 9.	Balance of school, home and community activities	M 1. Belief in development of whole self, including a healthy balance of mental, social/emotional, and physical well-being
B-SMS 10.	Ability to manage transitions and adapt to change	M 3. Positive attitude toward work and learning M 4. Self-confidence in ability to succeed M 5. Belief in using abilities to their fullest to achieve high-quality results and outcomes
B-SS 1.	Effective oral and written communication skills and listening skills	M 1. Belief in development of whole self, including a healthy balance of mental, social/emotional, and physical well-being M 4. Self-confidence in ability to succeed
B-SS 2.	Positive, respectful and supportive relationships with students who are similar to and different from them	M 2. Sense of acceptance, respect, support and inclusion for self and others in the school environment M 3. Positive attitude toward work and learning

	Behavior Standard	Mindset Standards
B-SS 3.	Positive relationships with adults to support success	M 2. Sense of acceptance, respect, support and inclusion for self and others in the school environment M 3. Positive attitude toward work and learning
B-SS 4.	Empathy	M 1. Belief in development of whole self, including a healthy balance of mental, social/emotional, and physical well-being M 2. Sense of acceptance, respect, support and inclusion for self and others in the school environment
B-SS 5.	Ethical decision-making and social responsibility	M 2. Sense of acceptance, respect, support and inclusion for self and others in the school environment M 4. Self-confidence in ability to succeed M 5. Belief in using abilities to their fullest to achieve high-quality results and outcomes
B-SS 6.	Effective collaboration and cooperation skills	M 1. Belief in development of whole self, including a healthy balance of mental, social/emotional, and physical well-being M 2. Sense of acceptance, respect, support and inclusion for self and others in the school environment M 5. Belief in using abilities to their fullest to achieve high-quality results and outcomes
B-SS 7.	Leadership and teamwork skills to work effectively in diverse groups	M 2. Sense of acceptance, respect, support and inclusion for self and others in the school environment M 3. Positive attitude toward work and learning M 4. Self-confidence in ability to succeed
B-SS 8.	Advocacy skills for self and others and ability to assert self, when necessary	M 1. Belief in development of whole self, including a healthy balance of mental, social/emotional, and physical well-being M 4. Self-confidence in ability to succeed
B-SS 9.	Social maturity and behaviors appropriate to the situation and environment	M 1. Belief in development of whole self, including a healthy balance of mental, social/emotional, and physical well-being M 4. Self-confidence in ability to succeed

	Behavior Standard	Mindset Standards
B-SS 10.	Cultural awareness, sensitivity and responsiveness	M 1. Belief in development of whole self, including a healthy balance of mental, social/emotional, and physical well-being M 2. Sense of acceptance, respect, support and inclusion for self and others in the school environment

Mindset Standards Connected to Behavior Standards

Mindset Standards	Behavior Standards			
M 1.	Belief in development of whole self, including a healthy balance of mental, social/emotional, and physical well-being	B-LS 1. B-LS 2. B-LS 6. B-LS 7. B-LS 10.	B-SMS 5. B-SMS 8. B-SMS 9.	B-SS 1. B-SS 4. B-SS 6. B-SS 8. B-SS 9. B-SS 10.
M 2.	Sense of acceptance, respect, support and inclusion for self and others in the school environment	B-LS 10.	B-SMS 8.	B-SS 1. B-SS 2. B-SS 3. B-SS 4. B-SS 5. B-SS 6. B-SS 7. B-SS 10.
M 3.	Positive attitude toward work and learning	B-LS 3. B-LS 4. B-LS 6. B-LS 8.	B-SMS 3. B-SMS 4. B-SMS 5. B-SMD 6. B-SMS 7. B-SMS 10.	B-SS 2 B-SS 3 B-SS 7
M 4.	Self-confidence in ability to succeed	B-LS 1. B-LS 2. B-LS 4. B-LS 7. B-LS 8. B-LS 10.	B-SMS 1. B-SMS 2. B-SMS 3. B-SMS 6. B-SMS 7. B-SMS 10.	B-SS 1. B-SS 5. B-SS 7. B-SS 8. B-SS 9.

Mindset Standards	Behavior Standards			
M 5.	Belief in using abilities to their fullest to achieve high-quality results and outcomes	B-LS 2. B-LS 3. B-LS 4. B-LS 5. B-LS 6. B-LS 7. B-LS 8. B-LS 9.	SMS 1. SMS 3. SMS 5. SMS 5. SMS 8. SMS 10.	B-SS 5. B-SS 6. B-SS 7.
M 6.	Understanding that postsecondary education and lifelong learning are necessary for long-term career success	B-LS 1. B-LS 3. B-LS 4. B-LS 5. B-LS 6. B-LS 7. B-LS 8. B-LS 9.	B-SMS 1. B-SMS 2. B-SMS 3. B-SMS 4. B-SMS 5.	

CHAPTER 3

Behavior Standards: Learning Strategies

Behavior standards include behaviors commonly associated with being a successful student. These are the visible, outward signs that a student is engaged and putting forth effort to learn. The behaviors are grouped into three subcategories, the first of which is Learning Strategies.

Learning strategies are the processes and tactics students employ to aid in the cognitive work of thinking, remembering or learning. There are 10 learning strategies standards. Students will demonstrate the following standards through classroom lessons, activities and/or individual/small-group counseling.

B-LS 1. Critical-thinking skills to make informed decisions
B-LS 2. Creative approach to learning, tasks and problem solving
B-LS 3. Time-management, organizational and study skills
B-LS 4. Self-motivation and self-direction to learning
B-LS 5. Media and technology skills to enhance learning
B-LS 6. High-quality standards for tasks and activities
B-LS 7. Long- and short-term academic, career and social/emotional goals
B-LS 8. Engagement in challenging coursework
B-LS 9. Decision-making informed by gathering evidence, getting others' perspectives and recognizing personal bias
B-LS 10. Participation in enrichment and extracurricular activities

Learning strategies are the means and methods employed during study. It is how one works to think, remember or learn. Students who possess these needed strategies can engage academic behaviors to maximize learning (Farrington et al., 2012, p. 13).

"Teaching Adolescents to Become Learners," one of the key sources for the development of the ASCA Student Standards, identifies several takeaways:
■ Learning strategies are an important component in a chain of noncognitive factors that shape students' academic performance.

- Three categories of learning strategies were identified: cognitive strategies (rehearsal, organizational and elaboration), metacognitive strategies (planning, monitoring, regulation) and resource-oriented strategies (establishing helpful environment; sustaining appropriate levels of attention, organizing time and resources, and concentration)
- Learning strategies include metacognition, self-regulated learning, time management and goal setting. Metacognition and self-regulated learning are goal-oriented endeavors to learning.
- Effective learning occurs when students monitor personal processes, ascertain difficulties and make needed adjustments.
- Self-regulated learning includes making judgments about personal cognitive abilities; defining the learning task; assessing factors involved in a task, linking current task to experience/knowledge, determining the level of difficulty, setting goals (includes identifying and planning goal, giving consequences to self, identifying success), selecting appropriate cognitive strategies, employing the strategies, monitoring what happens.
- Judgment of learning is key to monitoring one's own thinking. It includes determining how much one has learned, deciding if one's level of learning is sufficient, knowing when more effort is needed.
- Learning strategies can be domain specific.
- Learning strategies can be taught.
- Effective learning strategies increase students' self-efficacy.
- The presence of learning strategies affects students' academic tenacity.
- Student motivation is connected to the use of learning strategies.

(Farrington et al., 2012).

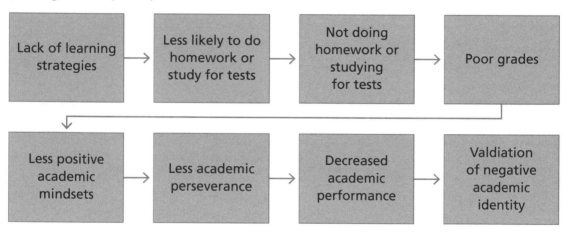

ASCA STUDENT STANDARDS: BEHAVIORS – LEARNING STRATEGIES

B-LS 1. Critical thinking skills to make informed decisions

Critical thinking is the process of analyzing facts objectively and forming a reasoned judgment. It may include accessing, interpreting and evaluating data sources and relevant facts; research; experiences; and observations of events. Good critical thinkers draw conclusions and discriminate between useful and useless points. It is the ability to think logically and derive helpful solutions. Examples of critical thinking skills include analysis, interpretation, inference, evaluation, explanation, self-regulation, open-mindedness and problem-solving.

Someone with critical thinking skills can be trusted to make independent decisions. A critical thinker can engage in reasoned debate, understanding the importance and relevance of specific arguments and ideas. Critical thinkers also recognize inconsistencies and errors in thinking in self and others.

Critical thinking abilities are important to learning and success in academic endeavors, and employers consider them a necessary skill in the workplace.

The mindsets foundational to this student standard are:
M 1. Belief in development of whole self, including a healthy balance of mental, social/emotional and physical well-being
M 4. Self-confidence in ability to succeed
M 6. Understanding that postsecondary education and lifelong learning are necessary for long-term success

Student Learning Objective Statements
You may choose to copy one of the objectives below, modify one to meet your plan more specifically or create your own. There is also a bank of objectives available in the learning objective database on the ASCA Student Standards website, *www.schoolcounselor.org/ mindsetsandbehaviors.*

This list of learning objectives is not exhaustive nor are the learning objectives listed in any special order. These are examples of student learning objectives linked to this standard. A few of the statements below offer options for refining the focus within the statement. You should select or define the appropriate focus when incorporating one of those statements.

Consider the context in which you'll deliver this information to students, as that may affect learning objective selection or creation. The setting can both enhance and limit certain activities and strategies. Knowing if you'll deliver this via small-group, classroom or large-group settings may guide your decision. In addition, the primary focus of the work, whether academic, career or social/emotional, aids in the selection/creation process. The primary domain in which the student standard is being addressed may help refine the objective.

Students will:
■ Analyze information for accuracy from a variety of sources.
■ Analyze scenarios to identify the primary problem or question.
■ Apply knowledge of personal goals and relevant postsecondary options to their own graduation/education plan.
■ Apply relevant information learned from a variety of sources to derive a solution.
■ Categorize data sources and how to access them for specific problems/questions.
■ Communicate ideas and solutions.
■ Create a personal rubric for selecting postsecondary option (environment, courses/degrees available, extracurricular opportunities, cost, distance from home, etc.)
■ Create solutions for a variety of scenarios.
■ Critique personal behaviors and level engagement in each of their classes.
■ Critique sources of information for possible bias.

- Determine three personal career/vocational possibilities and specify the relevant requirements for each.
- Determine which extracurricular club, activity or team best matches their preferences, skills and/or talents.
- Engage in respectful debate.
- Evaluate advertising images to distinguish fact and opinion and identify possible bias (portrayals that might be inaccurate, unhealthy or value-laden, as well as those that can be linked to any axis of privilege, oppression or intersectionality).
- Evaluate the impact of personal actions, behaviors and engagement on their own grades.
- Explain how to analyze data for accuracy.
- Generate a list of financial resources for career/vocational possibilities.
- Identify and define bias evident in information sources.
- Identify beliefs and assumptions in others.
- Identify personal beliefs and assumptions.
- Identify training/educational opportunities available at three postsecondary options.
- Illustrate the influences of personal experiences and opinions of others on personal beliefs and assumptions.
- Name questioning techniques.
- Name the steps for solving problems.
- Summarize different perspectives.

Strategies to use or suggest to teachers might include:
Practice seems to be the best way to develop critical thinking skills. Develop a series of problems/scenarios/dilemmas to provide that practice. Make these safe for student engagement and discussion by avoiding topics too deeply mired in religious, moral or political beliefs. Although those are important conversations, focus this practice on light-hearted, fun topics. Remember, the purpose is to practice the process.

Critical thinking improvement:
- Ask basic questions. What do you know and how do you know it? What might you be overlooking?
- Question basic assumptions. Reflect and evaluate what you believe and what you think you know.
- Be aware of your mental processes. Know your biases and personal prejudices and how they might be influencing your conclusions.
- Try reversing things. Change the order in which you are considering events, causes, information.
- Evaluate the existing evidence. Look at what others are doing. Is it working? How did they know to do it? How can I apply that to my needs?
- Think for yourself. Use what you can from the ideas of others but realize your own are also valuable.
- Realize no one thinks critically all the time. Recognize when it is required and work to use it. Accept that mistakes and misjudgments will occur and try to learn from them.

Steps of critical thinking include the following:
1. Identify the problem or question.
2. Gather data, opinions and arguments.

3. Analyze and evaluate the data.
4. Identify assumptions.
5. Establish significance.
6. Decide or reach a conclusion.

B-LS 2. Creative approach to learning tasks and problem solving

Creativity is the use of the imagination or original ideas. It may include perceiving problems/events/situations in new ways, finding previously hidden patterns, making new connections between information or occurrences and crafting solutions. Creativity may generate concepts (ideas, theories, music) or things (artwork, inventions, writings). Psychology Today adds that creativity does not need to be "grand and inspiring," but is also evident in the "daily acts of ingenuity and novel workarounds" (n.d.-a, para. 2).

Foundational Mindsets

The mindsets foundational to this student standard include:

M 1. Belief in development of whole self, including a healthy balance of mental, social/emotional and physical well-being

M 4. Self-confidence in ability to succeed

M 5. Belief in using abilities to their fullest to achieve high-quality results and outcomes

Student Learning Objective Statements

You may choose to copy one of the objectives below, modify one to meet your plan more specifically or create your own. There is also a bank of objectives available in the ASCA Student Standards learning objective database.

This list of learning objectives is not exhaustive, nor are the objectives listed in any special order. These are examples of student learning objectives linked to this standard. A few of the statements below offer options for refining the focus within the statement. You should select or define the appropriate focus when incorporating one of those statements.

Consider the context in which you'll deliver this information to students, as that may affect learning objective selection or creation. The setting can both enhance and limit certain activities and strategies. Knowing if you'll deliver this via small-group, classroom or large-group settings may guide your decision. In addition, the primary focus of the work, whether academic, career or social/emotional, aids in the selection/creation process. The primary domain in which the student standard is being addressed may help refine the objective.

Students will:
- Characterize essential themes in college application (or scholarship) essays.
- Compose an image (or poem, song, essay, etc.) depicting different definitions of success.
- Create "mind maps" connecting different ideas, thoughts, opinions, relationships and understanding those connections.
- Create a career map with a designated life goal (destination) along with personal skills and talents, necessary training and/or education needed and potential barriers.
- Create visual representations to clarify ideas, thoughts and feelings.
- Define creativity.

- Describe how personal ideas, opinions and beliefs affect one's presentation of those ideas, opinions and beliefs.
- Describe one's own thoughts and beliefs that may limit personal creativity.
- Describe one's own patterns for study and how they help or hinder academic success.
- Design a vision board portraying personal life outcomes (career, work, lifestyle, etc.).
- Develop a personal plan for success to use for classes in which they are currently underperforming.
- Diagram contributions to a specific peer group, school class or school.
- Engage in brief "thought breaks" (mind vacations, chair yoga poses, mindfulness activities, etc.).
- Engage in reflection activities following learning activities (journaling, artistic doodling/drawing, mandalas, etc.).
- Explain connections between thoughts, behaviors and actions with school success.
- Express ideas, thoughts, opinions and beliefs in ways they can be heard by others.
- Express personal feelings in a variety of ways that limit escalation of feelings or conflicts.
- Identify a variety of study methods that enhance learning.
- Identify how personal ideas, opinions and beliefs influence one's own thinking.
- Illustrate how study habits and patterns influence grades.
- Illustrate personal affirmations that challenge/dispute their own negative thoughts.
- Interpret social interactions to identify options that might change the outcome.
- List personal ideas, thoughts, opinions and beliefs.
- Perceive situations from different perspectives.
- Summarize the ideas, thoughts, opinions, beliefs of others.

Strategies to use or suggest to teachers might include:
Creativity can be learned and may be facilitated by:
- Environments that offer safety for the exploration and expression of new ideas
- Opportunities to collaborate
- Exposure to novel experiences and learning
- Engaging in artistic expression for reflection and exploration
- Changing routines
- Giving attention to moments and opportunities to think about or do things differently
- Taking a break (rest, distraction, mindfulness activities)
- Mapping of connections between ideas and recognizing relationships

B-LS 3. Time-management, organizational and study skills

When addressing this learning strategy, it is important to begin by discerning exactly what students' specific problems are. For example, study skills represent a broad array of skills and tend to be content-specific; students need different skills for math class than for language arts. Time management involves different skill sets, so it is necessary to determine which skills students are missing from their repertoire. Organization is an overarching concept that affects all students. Taking the time to determine which areas and/or skills individual students need the most help with will result in a well-targeted intervention with an increased chance of having a positive impact on student outcomes.

Foundational Mindsets

The mindsets foundational to this student standard include:

M 3. Positive attitude toward work and learning

M 6. Understanding that postsecondary education and lifelong learning are necessary for long-term success

M 5. Belief in using abilities to their fullest to achieve high-quality results and outcomes

Student Learning Objective Statements

You may choose to copy one of the objectives below, modify one to meet your plan more specifically or create your own. There is also a bank of objectives available in the learning objective database on the ASCA Student Standards learning objectives database.

This list of learning objectives is not exhaustive nor are the objectives listed in any special order. These are examples of student learning objectives linked to this standard. A few of the statements below offer options for refining the focus within the statement. You should select or define the appropriate focus when incorporating one of those statements.

Consider the context in which you'll deliver this information to students, as that may affect learning objective selection or creation. The setting can both enhance and limit certain activities and strategies. Knowing if you'll deliver this via small-group, classroom or large-group settings may guide your decision. In addition, the primary focus of the work, whether academic, career or social/emotional, aids in the selection/creation process. The primary domain in which the student standard is being addressed may help refine the objective.

Students will:
- Analyze relationship between time spent studying and final product/grades.
- Answer one or more questions in a class.
- Appraise their current skill level and determine skills needed for success in a specific endeavor (class, content area, project, etc.).
- Articulate personal thoughts, opinions and ideas in a group discussion.
- Ask one or more questions in a class.
- Complete necessary tasks/responsibilities within required time.
- Connect grades and test scores with motivation, effort, work completion, class participation, time spent studying and school engagement.
- Create a specific but flexible schedule ensuring schoolwork completion.
- Create an ordered list for how to complete a task.
- Create plans with intermittent deadlines for long-term tasks.
- Describe a variety of study skills (mnemonics, chunking, scheduling, utilizing resources, peer support, etc.).
- Develop a plan, with observable behavioral steps, that moves them toward academic achievement.
- Develop specific study tools (Cornell note taking process, graphic organizers, mind maps, etc.).
- Employ study skills (mnemonics, chunking, scheduling, utilizing resources, peer support, etc.).
- Establish an efficient workspace.
- Establish one academic goal requiring them to stretch their abilities and strengthen their work habits.

- Explain a variety of techniques for memorizing information (mnemonic devices, acronyms, put it to music, rhyming, peg system, use all senses, create a memory palace, chunking, create vivid visuals/images, write it down, write and erase, mind maps, memorize specific content starting at the end and working backward).
- Explain the benefit of reviewing what was learned in class/school daily.
- Identify resources that may provide support for addressing personal challenges.
- Identify what is needed in an efficient workshop.
- Initiate challenging school tasks with minimal prompting.
- Label task completion challenges (multitasking, perfectionistic thinking, inappropriate focus on unimportant detail, time wasters, poor organization, etc.).
- Maintain all school materials so they are accessible for use.
- Predict amount of time required for specific school tasks.
- Predict possible barriers to class or school success.
- Prioritize multiple school tasks.
- Recognize task avoidance behaviors.
- Understand how and when to use a variety of graphic organizers.
- Use organizational tools for school (agendas, to-do lists, calendars, etc.).
- Use time-management tools (agendas, to-do lists, calendars, etc.).

Strategies to use or suggest to teachers might include:
- Provide instruction on using time-management tools, including to-do lists, time audit, activity log or diary, to determine how you spend your time; school agendas; calendars (daily, weekly, monthly); daily schedules.
- Provide instruction on how to establish priorities, including learning to distinguish importance of various tasks/responsibilities, how to manage conflicting priorities and how to accurately judge time required for various tasks/responsibilities.
- Provide instruction on maintaining focus, including identifying personal distractors and focus enhancers; creating work environments to limit distractions; knowing how to focus with distractions and competing interests; knowing and utilizing personal productive times of day.
- Provide instruction on specific organizational tools and strategies: color coding, effective labeling, storage options for school materials, resources, electronic data, desk and notebook organization, school agendas, calendars, graphic organizers, etc.
- Provide instruction on the specific skills needed to learn, practice and remember information (effective reading practices for learning, note-taking systems, creating study aids, information review strategies, mnemonic devices for remembering information, SQ3R, Cornell notetaking, help-seeking skills, self-monitoring, etc.).

B-LS 4. Self-motivation and self-direction to learning
Motivation is often discussed and debated in education. It is important for school counselors to reflect on their own beliefs about motivation, where and how it originates, and how they can foster it in students.

The issue of extrinsic versus intrinsic motivation is a common focus of educational discussions and research. Extrinsic motivation involves external rewards. Intrinsic motivation comes from within the individual and is the satisfaction experienced from accomplishing a task.

Author Daniel Pink describes the potential dangers associated with contingent rewards, which are delivered when a specific task is completed. They tend to produce an initial, brief surge of motivation that isn't sustained over time. The rewards move the focus toward the product and away from the process, which is specifically problematic when learning is involved. The focus on the final reward may also encourage unethical actions. If used, rewards should be unexpected and infrequent. The secret to true motivation is autonomy, mastery and purpose. Humans want to direct their own lives, learn, create new things and improve ourselves and the world (Pink, 2011).

Alfie Kohn (2018), author of "Punished by Rewards," continues to report that "Rewards are Still Bad News." Consistent evidence substantiates rewards diminish interest, effort and excellence.

There are multiple studies illustrating that school attendance that may improve when rewards are given returns to earlier patterns of absences when the rewards are dropped. One study out of Harvard (Shafer, 2019) examined the school attendance of 15,000 students and found that the rewards had no effect or led to poorer attendance.

Remember that intrinsic motivation is key to student success. Intrinsic motivation includes fascination with the subject, a sense of relevance to life and the world, a sense of accomplishment in mastering it and a sense of calling to it (Delong & Winter, 2002). Furthermore, intrinsic motivation is undermined by external rewards and punishments. Kohn says that intrinsic motivation "is the best predictor of high-quality achievement" and that "people promised a reward for doing something often end up doing it more poorly." (Kohn, 2018, para 3.)

So, what exactly does motivate students? Self-motivation can be described as doing what needs to be done without influence from others. It is the individual's capacity for finding reason and will to complete a task in face of challenges, distractions, task difficulties, competing interests, discouragement and frustrations without giving up or external prompts to continue. It includes initiating, maintaining commitment and effort, and persevering until complete.

The relationship between the student and the teacher is critical to student motivation. When that relationship is positive, students are more motivated academically. In addition, four qualities have been identified as critical for increasing student motivation:
- Autonomy: students experience choice and feel empowered to manage their own learning
- Competence: students believe they can be successful
- Relatedness: students feel connected to their teacher and to classmates
- Relevance: students understand the importance of the task or content

Foundational Mindsets
The mindsets foundational to this student standard include:
M 3. Positive attitude toward work and learning
M 4. Self-confidence in ability to succeed
M 5. Belief in using abilities to their fullest to achieve high-quality results and outcomes
M 6. Understanding that postsecondary education and lifelong learning are necessary for long-term success

Student Learning Objective Statements

You may choose to copy one of the objectives below, modify one to meet your plan more specifically or create your own. There is also a bank of objectives available in the ASCA Student Standards learning objectives database.

This list of learning objectives is not exhaustive nor are the objectives listed in any special order. These are examples of student learning objectives linked to this standard. A few of the statements below offer options for refining the focus within the statement. You should select or define the appropriate focus when incorporating one of those statements.

Consider the context in which you'll deliver this information to students, as that may affect learning objective selection or creation. The setting can both enhance and limit certain activities and strategies. Knowing if you'll deliver this via small-group, classroom or large-group settings may guide your decision. In addition, the primary focus of the work, whether academic, career or social/emotional, aids in the selection/creation process. The primary domain in which the student standard is being addressed may help refine the objective.

Students will:
- Adhere to classroom norms.
- Analyze thoughts for rational/irrational beliefs.
- Articulate their personal reasons for working to succeed in school.
- Classify resources for academic help.
- Define positive academic behaviors.
- Demonstrate positive academic behaviors (regular and prompt attendance, active class participation, seeking help when needed, etc.).
- Describe ways in which content areas are interesting.
- Develop a personal vision statement for their desired life outcomes.
- Engage in classroom tasks and discussions.
- Explain how motivation affects effort, work completion, class participation, time studying and school engagement.
- Give examples of required/relevant learning across the lifespan.
- Identify learning resources/supports (media center, tutoring services, after-school homework help, homework help line, study groups, internet resources, etc.).
- Initiate school tasks with limited prompts.
- List pros and cons for attending school regularly.
- Locate learning opportunities in the school (high-rigor courses, academic clubs, etc.).
- Modify personal negative self-talk, faulty thinking or capacity-limiting thoughts.
- Name specific ways in which they contribute to their peer group, class and/or school.
- Persist through academic tasks.
- State academic strengths and growth areas.
- Summarize ways in which they contribute to their class.

Strategies to use or suggest to teachers might include:

Jennifer Gonzalez (2016) identifies five questions to ask yourself when dealing with unmotivated students:
1. How is my relationship with my students?
2. How much choice do my students have?

3. Am I relying heavily on carrots and sticks?
4. Do my words contribute to a growth mindset or a fixed mindset?
5. What am I doing to make the content relevant to my students' lives?

Take time to discover what motivates students. Consider that socially linked motivators tend to be more effective and cheaper than tangible treats. Choice is a powerful motivator. Create environments in which students experience freedom of choice. This autonomy may include choice on where one sits in the classroom (organizational choice), how one will complete an academic assignment or what kind of practice/assignment will meet each student's academic needs (procedural choice). Cognitive choice, through which students generate solutions via small-group work, respond to some problem or issue presented (Ferlazzo, 2015).

Create environments in which feedback is delivered in ways that build students' sense of competence. Strategies to establish this type of environment typically including focusing on process over product. In addition, learning occurs best when the ratio of positive-to-negative feedback falls between 3-1 and 5-1. Even the feedback language of "and" and "what if" rather than "but" encourages greater effort (Ferlazzo, 2015).

Teacher-student relationships are critical to motivation. Create environments in which relatedness is evident. Relationships are key to student intrinsic motivation. Ferlazzo (2015) built on Marzano's work to develop four suggestions for school adults:
1. Be interested in your students
2. Act friendly
3. Stay flexible
4. Do not give up on students

Create environments in which relevance is intentionally stated. It is most effective for students to generate personal connections between class learning and life, rather than simply having the teachers state connections. Focus some assignments on how students perceive what they are learning and how that affects their lives.

Students must believe they can improve in order to persist at any task. Students' beliefs in their own capacity are influenced by grading practices, perceived safety to make mistakes in the classroom and an emphasis on process over product. Classrooms that value the learning process, make mistakes a normal part of that process and focus on mastery of skills and knowledge over grades on assessments support students' motivation.

The National Board for Professional Teaching Standards identifies five strategies for motivating students (Wilcox, 2018).
1. Promote growth mindset over fixed mindset. Acknowledge and commend hard work and effort. Incorporate quick and easy formative assessments. Offer opportunity for students to provide feedback on the teacher.
2. Develop meaningful and respectful relationships with your students. Get to know your students. Include a routine of taking five minutes to share good news.
3. Grow a community of learners in your classroom. The classroom environment must be safe so students are comfortable with taking risks and making mistakes. Establish class

norms that encourage students supporting each other, making learning struggles acceptable and normalized. Incorporate cooperative group work. Proudly display student work.

4. Establish high expectations and establish clear goals. Ensure the expectations are clear and consistent and provide the support to realize them. Daily learning goals are especially effective when routinely posted.
5. Be inspirational.

B-LS 5. Media and technology skills to enhance learning

Technology is both a ubiquitous component and essential tool for students' educational experiences. Students need to develop technology skills, learn authorship rules, understand how to access online information and learn online social responsibility. In addition, information literacy, media literacy and technology literacy have been identified as part of 21st-century skills (Trilling & Fadel, 2012). Students must be able to safely navigate and discern all forms of digital technology. This standard focuses on the uses of media and technology by our students.

Foundational Mindsets

The mindsets foundational to this student standard include:

M 3. Positive attitude toward work and learning

M 5. Belief in using abilities to their fullest to achieve high-quality results and outcomes

Student Learning Objective Statements

You may choose to copy one of the objectives below, modify one to meet your plan more specifically or create your own. There is also a bank of objectives available in the ASCA Student Standards learning objectives database.

This list of learning objectives is not exhaustive nor are the objectives listed in any special order. These are examples of student learning objectives linked to this standard. A few of the statements below offer options for refining the focus within the statement. You should select or define the appropriate focus when incorporating one of those statements.

Consider the context in which you'll deliver this information to students, as that may affect learning objective selection or creation. The setting can both enhance and limit certain activities and strategies. Knowing if you'll deliver this via small-group, classroom or large-group settings may guide your decision. In addition, the primary focus of the work, whether academic, career or social/emotional, aids in the selection/creation process. The primary domain in which the student standard is being addressed may help refine the objective.

Students will:
- Access and interpret information from student portals (grades, assignments, feedback, etc.).
- Appraise multiple media sources for researching postsecondary options.
- Define essential technology skills required for educational experiences.
- Demonstrate responsible technology use.
- Develop multimedia presentations around career options (postsecondary options, college options, training options).

- Employ available technology resources enabling college-, career- and life-planning.
- Examine multiple media sources for information on postsecondary processes and requirements.
- Explain rules of etiquette for email communications.
- Explain the school's rules for technology and social media.
- Formulate a personal plan for managing online bullying.
- Generate a list of technology resources for enhancing own learning.
- Identify guidelines for establishing a healthy, respected online presence.
- Identify guidelines for responsible technology use.
- Integrate information from multiple media sources to make informed decisions on how to pay for postsecondary options.
- Investigate laws related to social media and use of technology.
- Organize financial requirements for preferred postsecondary options.
- Organize information on general postsecondary/college/career processes and requirements.
- Record evidence of postsecondary/college/career options from multiple media sources.
- Research how to get support for tech problems.
- Use multiple media sources for gathering specific information on career options (education/training/performance requirements, job outlook, job conditions and benefits).

Strategies to use or suggest to teachers might include:
Incorporate strategies in lessons and activities so students:
- Create multimedia presentations
- Find and insert relevant videos
- Search and find information
- Engage in interpersonal computing by completing assignments using cloud environments
- Understand safety rules and procedures

B-LS 6. High-quality standards for tasks and activities
Setting high-quality standards relates to students' willingness to devote the necessary time and effort to a school task or assignment. Individual students can determine their own "high standard," as this definition is personal and somewhat subject to skills, talents and interests. Setting those personal standards is affected by one's own self-efficacy beliefs, the influences of those one routinely associates with and one's own willingness to engage in opportunities that stretch one's capacity.

Foundational Mindsets
The mindsets foundational to this student standard include:
M 1. Belief in development of whole self, including a healthy balance of mental, social/emotional and physical well-being
M 3. Positive attitude toward work and learning
M 5. Belief in using abilities to their fullest to achieve high-quality results and outcomes
M 6. Understanding that postsecondary education and lifelong learning are necessary for long-term success

Student Learning Objective Statements

You may choose to copy one of the objectives below, modify one to meet your plan more specifically or create your own. There is also a bank of objectives available in the ASCA Student Standards learning objectives database.

This list of learning objectives is not exhaustive nor are the objectives listed in any special order. These are examples of student learning objectives linked to this standard. A few of the statements below offer options for refining the focus within the statement. You should select or define the appropriate focus when incorporating one of those statements.

Consider the context in which you'll deliver this information to students, as that may affect learning objective selection or creation. The setting can both enhance and limit certain activities and strategies. Knowing if you'll deliver this via small-group, classroom or large-group settings may guide your decision. In addition, the primary focus of the work, whether academic, career or social/emotional, aids in the selection/creation process. The primary domain in which the student standard is being addressed may help refine the objective.

Students will:
- Assess one's own responsibility for learning in differing classes, regardless of relationship with the teacher, the course content and/or personal ambitions.
- Compare different definitions of success.
- Compile a variety of definitions of "quality work."
- Complete assignments in full and on time.
- Correlate postsecondary options to career and life outcomes.
- Create weekly schedules to maximize study time.
- Define the benefits of continued learning/education/training across the lifespan.
- Describe the learning process (mistakes, growth, editing processes, etc.).
- Differentiate personal skills/talents/knowledge in different classes and at different time frames (to recognize growth).
- Distinguish tasks requiring additional effort based on weight of assignments.
- Enumerate what is required to produce quality work.
- Establish a weekly goal for submitting an identified number of assignments meeting established high standards.
- Establish personal mile-markers for reaching one's life aspirations.
- Explain the benefits of a growth mindset.
- Identify academic outcomes if quality work is routinely submitted.
- Produce high-quality work.
- Recognize which academic tasks are especially important.
- Retell personal stories of success when encountering challenges and setbacks.
- Understand the difference between performance goals and mastery goals.
- Write a personal definition for success.
- Write an academic mastery goal, goal plan and progress monitoring plan for one class.

Strategies to use or suggest to teachers might include:
- Help students explore and identify personal values and beliefs about schoolwork and task completion. Discuss students' perceptions of the relevance and significance of specific tasks and specific content areas.

- Help students authentically evaluate their expectations. Individuals tend to inflate or underestimate personal capacities. For example, a student who is failing all classes may expect to pass everything next semester or determine that nothing will help or change that failure rate. Either expectation can paralyze the student's ability to work different-ly. Balancing too high and too low with reality can be challenging and must be gently managed; yet it is necessary to arrive at a place of high standards that stretch without breaking a student's sense of self.
- Help students manage their fears associated with establishing these high standards. Do-ing well one time means others expect you to do well next time, which can be daunting for students. Develop ways for students to continue working while acknowledging their fears without becoming ruled by them.
- Explore students' individual stories that make up their own identity. Help them deter-mine any underlying experiences or beliefs that may be limiting their success. Automatic negative thoughts are an example of cognitive limits.
- Help students identify realistic outcomes. Describe what might happen if those person-alized standards for quality are achieved and how that might feel. Describe what might occur if those standards are not met. Drive a realistic probability for outcomes.
- Use solution-focused techniques, emphasizing the search for exceptions.
- Use cognitive behavior theory techniques that challenge errors in thinking.

B-LS 7. Long- and short-term academic, career and social/emotional goals

Goal work is crucial to school and life success. Creating and working to achieve goals helps students learn the skills of planning, organizing and time management while building confi-dence and self-efficacy. Goal work facilitates increased skills in planning, setting priorities and delaying gratification; students experience increased hope and optimism as goals are realized.

Goal work also affects motivation, as the narrow focus of a well-crafted goal maintains the individual's focus on a specific component while ultimately affecting the bigger picture. The smaller focus makes it more manageable and less overwhelming. When the goal is achieved, feeling success is experienced, which in turn, generates more successes.

Goal work teaches students to self-monitor their own progress. This work increases stu-dents' awareness of how much they've accomplished and what they still have left to do. Goal setting can also provide a challenge to students for whom some success comes easily. For these students, creating a goal that stretches beyond the class expectations keeps them engaged and motivated to work in the content area.

Foundational Mindsets
The mindsets foundational to this student standard include:
M 1. Belief in development of whole self, including a healthy balance of mental, social/ emotional, and physical well-being
M 3. Positive attitude toward work and learning
M 4. Self-confidence in ability to succeed
M 5. Belief in using abilities to their fullest to achieve high-quality results and outcomes
M 6. Understanding that postsecondary education and lifelong learning are necessary for long-term success

Student Learning Objective Statements

You may choose to copy one of the objectives below, modify one to meet your plan more specifically or create your own. There is also a bank of objectives available in the ASCA Student Standards learning objectives database.

This list of learning objectives is not exhaustive nor are the objectives listed in any special order. These are examples of student learning objectives linked to this standard. A few of the statements below offer options for refining the focus within the statement. You should select or define the appropriate focus when incorporating one of those statements.

Consider the context in which you'll deliver this information to students, as that may affect learning objective selection or creation. The setting can both enhance and limit certain activities and strategies. Knowing if you'll deliver this via small-group, classroom or large-group settings may guide your decision. In addition, the primary focus of the work, whether academic, career or social/emotional, aids in the selection/creation process. The primary domain in which the student standard is being addressed may help refine the objective.

Students will:
- Analyze the experiences of others who set and worked toward personal goals.
- Appraise goal progress and goal achievement.
- Articulate personal expectations for work and achievement.
- Connect current schoolwork (courses, tasks, extracurricular activities, etc.) to future opportunities.
- Connect goal work with improved academics, career and social/emotional outcomes.
- Construct a goal plan, with observable, behavioral steps, that moves them toward goal achievement.
- Create a presentation defining personal success.
- Develop postsecondary/college/career goals with all components of the SMART format.
- Develop short-term academic goals that include all components of the SMART format.
- Differentiate focus and attributes of performance goals and mastery goals.
- Explain how effort affects outcomes.
- Identify others who can and will support their goal work.
- Measure progress of an identified goal plan.
- Modify goal plans when encountering setbacks during goal work.
- Name and define components of a well-written goal statement (SMART).
- Predict job opportunities and/or salaries based on a variety of postsecondary/college/career options.
- Recognize obstacles and develop strategies for overcoming them.
- Write a long-term academic goal.
- Write a long-term career goal.
- Write a long-term social/emotional goal.
- Write a short-term academic goal.
- Write a short-term career goal.
- Write a short-term social/emotional goal.

Strategies to use or suggest to teachers might include:

- Teach students the difference between mastery and performance goals.
- Teach and support the entire goal process. It's more than simply writing a goal statement. It must include crafting a workable plan to achieve that goal and then routinely monitoring one's progress with that plan. Check in and talk about goal progress and barriers that might develop. Develop a concrete way to track progress. Celebrate goal completion.
- Allow sufficient time for goal work to occur. A semester or a school year might be appropriate for the goal work.
- Avoid temptation to link goal work to extrinsic rewards. Extrinsic rewards undermine motivation and devalue the goal.

B-LS 8. Engagement in challenging coursework

Students who are actively engaged are willing and able to take academic risks. They can identify the value of specific courses and content and can link them to future goals. They know how to participate appropriately and complete assigned tasks well and on time. They try hard and take pride in learning the material and incorporating it into their lives. Engagement involves attention, curiosity, interest and optimism, which then generates motivation to learn.

Student engagement is demonstrated in:
- Positive feelings about the teacher, class and school
- Sense of belonging in the class and school
- Attentive, active students
- Intrinsic motivation of students
- Self-regulation of students

Student engagement links to these conditions:
- A physical and psychologically safe environment
- Positive relationships with classmates, teachers and administrators
- Positive self-efficacy validated by others
- Teaching strategies that are interesting and foster curiosity
- Connections to real life
- Options in how they learn and demonstrate that learning
- Authentic and timely feedback

Foundational Mindsets
The mindsets which are foundational to this student standard include:
M 3. Positive attitude toward work and learning
M 4. Self-confidence in ability to succeed
M 5. Belief in using abilities to their fullest to achieve high-quality results and outcomes
M 6. Understanding that postsecondary education and lifelong learning are necessary for long-term success

Student Learning Objective Statements
You may choose to copy one of the objectives below, modify one to meet your plan more specifically or create your own. There is also a bank of objectives available in the ASCA Student Standards learning objectives website.

This list of learning objectives is not exhaustive nor are the objectives listed in any special order. These are examples of student learning objectives linked to this standard. A few of the statements below offer options for refining the focus within the statement. You should select or define the appropriate focus when incorporating one of those statements.

Consider the context in which you'll deliver this information to students, as that may affect learning objective selection or creation. The setting can both enhance and limit certain activities and strategies. Knowing if you'll deliver this via small-group, classroom or large-group settings may guide your decision. In addition, the primary focus of the work, whether academic, career or social/emotional, aids in the selection/creation process. The primary domain in which the student standard is being addressed may help refine the objective.

Students will:
- Analyze the link between student engagement and academic outcomes (grades, learning, etc.)
- Answer questions in class.
- Articulate specific behaviors associated with effective class participation, as defined by the course instructor (pay attention, take notes, listen, ask questions, answer questions, comply with requests, react appropriately to specific events/occurrences in the classroom).
- Ask questions in class.
- Construct an academic goal and plan for higher levels of achievement in grades and/or selected courses.
- Define the necessary attributes, coursework and level of school participation to be a competitive candidate for a preferred postsecondary/college/career opportunity.
- Develop a personal plan to acquire the necessary attributes, coursework and level of school participation to be a competitive candidate for a preferred postsecondary/college/career opportunity.
- Demonstrate awareness/knowledge of specific content for classroom discussions.
- Describe individual teachers' specific classroom expectations.
- Determine personal abilities supporting improved academic outcomes.
- Earn a competitive grade point average for identified postsecondary/college/career opportunities.
- Earn credits to graduate postsecondary/college/career ready.
- Employ planned strategies to enhance academic success in one specified course.
- Explain graduation credit requirements.
- Explain what student engagement in the classroom looks and sounds like.
- Give examples of benefits of engaging in one advanced course.
- Give examples of specific peer group influences and how they encourage/discourage school success.
- Initiate work assignments in class.
- Join two or more school clubs, activities and extracurricular activities.
- Match and select courses based on personal goals and relevant postsecondary options as part of a comprehensive graduation plan.
- Present succinct synopsis of postsecondary/career admission requirements.
- Substantiate taking academic risks as part of the learning process (e.g., attempting challenging tasks and courses, boosting effort on specific academic tasks, answering/asking questions in class, etc.).

- Summarize ways in which classmates demonstrate acknowledgement of and appreciation for shared ideas, opinions and thoughts.
- Summarize ways in which they contribute to the learning process in the classroom.

Strategies to use or suggest to teachers might include:
- Foster recognition of and value for process over product.
- Evaluate current incentive programs against research and demonstrated effectiveness for all.
- Review grading practices.
- Follow the 10:2 rule; for every 10 minutes of instruction, allow two minutes to process, reflect, respond.
- Allow 5-7 seconds of "think time" when asking questions
- Incorporate movement.
- Pick up the pace.
- Summarize lessons using the 3-2-1 method: record three things they learned, two interesting things and one question they now have.
- Provide professional development to faculty and staff for building community in the classroom and/or building positive relationships with students.
- Consider using restorative justice practices.
- Administer and analyze results of student climate surveys or student engagement surveys.
- Analyze enrollment patterns of students in special education, remediation, gifted and advanced placements. Research alternatives for increasing enrollment in challenging courses.

B-LS 9. Decision-making informed by gathering evidence, getting others' perspectives and recognizing personal bias.

Good decision-making is essential for life success and a desired trait by future employers. It is a necessary and complex process that must be taught and practiced.

This standard addresses more than simple decision-making, although that is an essential piece. It also includes the collection of authentic information from quality resources and the ability to consider the problem from variable perspectives. Each of the three facets carry their own significance.

Gathering evidence requires the identification of accurate resources, an especially relevant skill for today's world in which information is so instantly available. The associated skill is the ability to discern which resources are reliable. Evidence gathering may also depend on the individual's ability to accurately interpret corrective feedback. As decisions are typically linked to specific dilemmas or difficulties, other stakeholders may offer opinions or even commands on what must be done. The individual must be able to filter the message from authorities, interpret it correctly and then determine how/if to incorporate. For example, a student may be facing postsecondary options and the associated decisions. Multiple resources may flood the student with information on various programs and opportunities, while teachers, coaches and family deliver their own expectations around what they think is the student's best choice. The student must decide which resources and voices carry the best, most accurate evidence.

Perspective taking adds complexities, as it requires the individual to think from another viewpoint. One coach may evaluate postsecondary options based on athletic reputation of an institution, while another is considering the probability of getting actual playing time. Teachers may be thinking about the instructional programs and what best matches a student's interests beyond sports. Meanwhile, family may be concerned about distance from home, finances and campus influences. Friends may attempt to persuade the student to their own future sites so that the friendships may continue beyond high school. When perspectives include other variables of culture, lifestyle, values, etc., it becomes even more complex.

Teaching a specific model and practicing that model will strengthen students' capacity for making the best possible informed decision. Most decision models include a series of steps with accompanying processes and resources for each. Steps may include:

1. Identify or frame the problem
2. Consider possible responses
3. Identify the consequences of each possible response
4. Weight the identified consequences
5. Research any additional information needed to make a choice
6. Select one of the possible solutions
7. Commit to the action

Foundational Mindsets
The mindsets foundational to this student standard include:

M 5. Belief in using abilities to their fullest to achieve high-quality results and outcomes

M 6. Understanding that postsecondary education and lifelong learning are necessary for long-term success

Student Learning Objective Statements
You may choose to copy one of the objectives below, modify one to meet your plan more specifically or create your own. There is also a bank of objectives available in the ASCA Student Standards learning objectives database.

This list of learning objectives is not exhaustive nor are the objectives listed in any special order. These are examples of student learning objectives linked to this standard. A few of the statements below offer options for refining the focus within the statement. You should select or define the appropriate focus when incorporating one of those statements.

Consider the context in which you'll deliver this information to students, as that may affect learning objective selection or creation. The setting can both enhance and limit certain activities and strategies. Knowing if you'll deliver this via small-group, classroom or large-group settings may guide your decision. In addition, the primary focus of the work, whether academic, career or social/emotional, aids in the selection/creation process. The primary domain in which the student standard is being addressed may help refine the objective.

Students will:
- Analyze resources for information for accuracy.
- Compare traditional and nontraditional paths for postsecondary options.
- Contrast how different individuals may experience similar circumstances or events.

- Create a personal rubric for evaluating postsecondary options.
- Critique advertising messages targeted to their demographic.
- Defend others' perspectives around a specific issue.
- Define personal values, beliefs and life goals.
- Demonstrate accepted standards for respectful discourse in conversations and collaborations with diverse peers.
- Determine course selection/enrollment based on desired postsecondary options.
- Evaluate postsecondary options against personal goals, skills, talents, preferred lifestyles and available resources.
- Evaluate responses against gathered evidence, varied perspectives, and personal values and goals to determine the best response.
- Explain the purpose and method of advertising messages.
- Explain their unique collection of abilities and attributes supporting improved academic outcomes.
- Identify a decision-making model.
- Identify how personal bias may influence information provided by others.
- Interpret information from authentic resources relevant to a specific issue.
- Restate others' perspectives on values, beliefs and goals.
- Specify a system for organizing evidence gathered from multiple sources around specific issues or topic.
- Summarize a process for gathering information and perspectives for the decision-making model.
- Tell how personal bias may influence how information is interpreted.

Strategies to use or suggest to teachers might include:
- Provide explicit teaching on a preferred decision-making model. There are many approaches and models available. Various graphic organizers also facilitate the use of a model.
- Incorporate decision-making models into varied situations and discussions as they develop. It can become part of many counseling sessions, classroom instruction and group experiences. Remembering to employ the model taught beyond the instruction is important.
- Provide instruction on how to determine the authenticity of information resources (electronic, media, friends, family, etc.).
- Provide instruction on how to discern the relevance and appropriateness of information gathered by good resources.
- Ensure that all work honors diversity and supports a variety of perspectives.
- Use literature and media as platforms to begin discussions on gathering evidence, evaluating evidence, considering perspectives and making decisions.

B-LS 10. Participation in enrichment and extracurricular activities

Enrichment and extracurricular activities are school- or community-sponsored programs and clubs occurring outside the regular school day. They allow students to navigate groups and build social skills, build self-confidence and explore various interests. In addition, participation strengthens students' connections in the school, a critical ingredient to school success. Opportunities may include dance, music, drama, debate, STEM, sports, service-learning, hobby clubs, youth organizations, fields of study and college majors, careers and more.

There are many benefits of students participating in these activities. Benefits include improved academic performance, exploration of interests and perspectives, enhanced self-confidence, broader social opportunities, productive breaks for schoolwork, development of essential life skills, and stronger resumes and university applications.

While considering these positive benefits, it is necessary to also be aware of who can access these opportunities and, more importantly, who cannot. Schools must find ways to increase access to programs so all students can participate.

Reflect on your school practices.
- Who gets selected to be a student helper, a new student guide or student ambassador?
- Who is not participating in extracurricular activities or enrichment?
- Why are some students not engaged?
- When are special programs, activities or clubs offered? Does the scheduling of these events limit student participation to those with independent transportation?
- What resources are needed for students to participate? Consider money, transportation, special supplies, adult/peer support, etc.
- Where do these activities occur? Are those sites accessible to all students? Consider location, environment, etc.
- How do we modify delivery of the activities to increase accessibility for all students?

Foundational Mindsets
The mindsets foundational to this student standard include:
M 1. Belief in development of whole self, including a healthy balance of mental, social/emotional, and physical well-being
M 2. Sense of acceptance, respect, support and inclusion for self and others in the school environment
M 4. Self-confidence in ability to succeed

Student Learning Objective Statements
You may choose to copy one of the objectives below, modify one to meet your plan more specifically or create your own. There is also a bank of objectives available in the ASCA Student Standards learning objectives database.

This list of learning objectives is not exhaustive nor are the objectives listed in any special order. These are examples of student learning objectives linked to this standard. A few of the statements below offer options for refining the focus within the statement. You should select or define the appropriate focus when incorporating one of those statements.

Consider the context in which you'll deliver this information to students, as that may affect learning objective selection or creation. The setting can both enhance and limit certain activities and strategies. Knowing if you'll deliver this via small-group, classroom or large-group settings may guide your decision. In addition, the primary focus of the work, whether academic, career or social/emotional, aids in the selection/creation process. The primary domain in which the student standard is being addressed may help refine the objective.

Students will:
- Advocate for personal access (or access for all) for engagement in specific school activities.
- Apply strategies to deal with any barriers to participation in enrichment/extracurricular activities.
- Classify the available enrichment and extracurricular activities into yes/maybe/no chart based on personal criteria for engagement.
- Compare and contrast personal interests, talents and/or skills with school clubs, activities and extracurricular activities.
- Complete one or more enrichment/extracurricular activities.
- Create a graphic organizer for possible extracurricular activities, identifying requirements, time commitments, accessibility, barriers, etc.
- Create a proposal for a new school club/activity/team that links to a personal interest/talent/skill.
- Determine barriers to participation in enrichment/extracurricular activities.
- Evaluate current school enrichment activities for possible engagement.
- Explain reasons to be involved in a specific enrichment or extracurricular activity.
- Explain what extracurricular and/or enrichment activities enhance students' postsecondary options.
- Explore reasons why some students are not engaged in enrichment and/or extracurricular activities.
- Identify personal skills/talents/interests.
- Identify which school activities will enhance one's own educational experience and future.
- List the benefits of participation in enrichment/extracurricular activities.
- Manage the demands of any selected enrichment/extracurricular activity with the demands of school coursework.
- Match personal skills, talents, interests and availability to one or more enrichment/extracurricular activities.
- Name five or more school clubs, activities and extracurricular activities and the requirements or expectations for each.
- Name the potential lifelong benefits of involvement with an enrichment or extracurricular activity.
- Prioritize personal interests, talents and/or skills.

Strategies to use or suggest to teachers might include:
- Deliver specific presentations that name and explain all enrichment and extracurricular activities to potential students prior to enrolling students.
- Create an online resource providing specific information for all available activities, how to become involved, expectations, timing, etc.
- Incorporate some clubs, interest groups and activities into the regular school day.
- Include discussion of participation in these activities in the graduation plan development.
- Deliver classroom presentations on the benefits of involvement in these activities.
- Identify students who may be appropriate for specific activities, and connect them to others who are already involved.
- Research grants and local community service clubs that might support accessibility for students.

Behavior Standards: Self-Management Skills

Behavior standards include behaviors commonly associated with being a successful student. These are the visible, outward signs that a student is engaged and putting forth effort to learn. The behaviors are grouped into three subcategories, the second of which is self-management skills.

B-SMS 1. Responsibility for self and actions
B-SMS 2. Self-discipline and self-control
B-SMS 3. Independent work
B-SMS 4. Delayed gratification for long-term rewards
B-SMS 5. Perseverance to achieve long- and short-term goals
B-SMS 6. Ability to identify and overcome barriers to learning
B-SMS 7. Effective coping skills
B-SMS 8. Balance of school, home and community activities

Self-management skills describe the continued focus on a goal despite obstacles (grit or persistence) and avoidance of distractions or temptations to prioritize higher pursuits over lower diversions (delayed gratification, self-discipline, self-control). Self-management also relates to student's ability to complete tasks independently, to monitor personal learning progress and to reinforce their own behavior. These skills enable and strengthen academic performance and productivity, increase time-on-task and have a positive impact on student outcomes. They continue to be a positive influence, facilitating success throughout life.

Chapter 4, Evidence on Academic Behaviors, of "Teaching Adolescents to Become Learners," one of the key sources for the development of the Mindsets & Behaviors, identifies several takeaways:

- Observed academic behaviors lead to inferences about students' attitudes, motivation and work effort toward school and learning.
- Academic perseverance includes both initial drive in a focused direction and the maintenance of that effort regardless of what happens.
- Academic perseverance is essential to achieving short- and long-term goals around educational achievement.

- An academically perseverant student is seen as one who is engaged, focused and persistent despite obstacles, setbacks and distractions.
- Academic tenacity enables students to withstand challenges and setbacks.
- Students' academic mindsets work to encourage or inhibit continuing effort.
- Grit is defined as a long-term quality that enables work, effort, interest and focus.
- Grit includes working strenuously toward challenges and maintaining effort and interest over years despite failure, adversity and plateaus in progress.
- Self-control is defined as the ability to avoid impulsive behaviors and fulfill short-term obligations.
- Self-control is tied to the ability to delay gratification, which includes resisting temptations and delaying treats/rewards.
- Self-control can be described as making repeated, immediate choices between options.
- Research and experiments demonstrate relationships between grit/self-control and students' grades, but the relationship strength varies based on how they are assessed.
- Academic perseverance, specifically, has been demonstrated to be responsive to interventions. (Farrington et al., 2012)

The specific skills associated with self-management include:
- Problem-solving
- Stress management
- Communication skills
- Time management (scheduling, planning, flexibility, creating to-do lists, time audits, prioritizing)
- Memory skills
- Healthy habits
- Knowing when to ask for help
- Assuming an active role in directing and engaging in learning
- Perseverance
- Ability to delay gratification
- Resistance to distractions, temptations, competing interests
- Ability to choose wisely and quickly, in the moment

B-SMS 1. Responsibility for self and others

Student responsibility emerges as students assume an active role in their learning and accept that they are accountable for their own academic success. Responsible students can be observed in behaviors that ensure their success, including:
- Attending class regularly, fully prepared and willing to actively participate.
- Self-advocating, often resulting in the side benefit of a stronger teacher-student relationship.
- Recognizing when they need help and being willing and able to ask questions.
- Communicating their needs and wants effectively and respectfully.
- Completing all school assignments and tasks, even when interest wanes or success seems remote.
- Finding ways to connect and relate to school content.
- Surrounding themselves with others who share a similar commitment to learning.
- Setting goals and working to achieve them.
- Planning their time and incorporating daily study time
- Keeping their commitments.

Foundational Mindsets

The mindsets foundational to this student standard include:

M 4. Self-confidence in ability to succeed

M 5. Belief in using abilities to their fullest to achieve high-quality results and outcomes

M 6. Understanding that postsecondary education and lifelong learning are necessary for long-term success

Student Learning Objective Statements

You may choose to copy one of the objectives below, modify to meet your plan more specifically, or create your own. There is also a bank of learning objectives available in the ASCA Student Standards learning objectives database.

This list of learning objectives is not exhaustive, nor are the objectives listed in any special order. These are examples of student learning objectives linked to this standard. A few of the statements below offer options for refining the focus within the statement. The school counselor should select or define the appropriate focus when incorporating one of those statements.

Consider the context in which this information will be delivered to students as that may impact the selection or creation of the learning objective. The setting can both enhance and limit certain activities and strategies. Knowing if this will be delivered via small group, classroom, or large group settings may guide the decision. In addition, the primary focus of the work, whether academic, career or social/emotional, aids in the selection/creation process. The primary domain in which the student standard is being addressed may help refine the objective.

Students will:
- Complete school assignments.
- Craft a plan for improving low grades in a class.
- Craft a plan for recovering lost credits.
- Create a plan based on observable behaviors to reach a short-term academic goal.
- Demonstrate identified study strategies in preparation for tests.
- Describe personal responsibilities for school experience and education.
- Describe the relationship between schoolwork, postsecondary options, job/vocational impact on lifestyle.
- Detail the most effective ways to study for tests.
- Determine connection between behaviors and outcomes.
- Develop ways to generate personal interest in course work and courses.
- Engage in productive conversations with school faculty and staff to enhance academic performance.
- Examine how behaviors affect outcomes.
- Explain how effort affects outcomes.
- Explain the influence of peers on their learning experience.
- Give examples for when and how to self-advocate.
- Identify class/teacher expectations.
- Investigate how course performance connects to future goals/aspirations.
- List possible consequences for failing to meet class/teacher expectations.

- Name consequences for dishonest work submission.
- Participate in challenging work.
- Perform extra tasks, responsibilities or assignments in response to unsatisfactory grades.
- Perform within class/teacher expectations.
- Practice specific behaviors identified in goal plans.
- Recognize when help is needed.
- Self-advocate for specific needs/wants.
- State consequences for incomplete or poorly performed work.
- State possible resources for academic support.
- Summarize steps for achieving a goal (writing, planning, monitoring, celebrating, etc.).
- Write a clear goal statement with a specific plan for how to achieve it.
- Write goal statements with all SMART components (specific, measurable, achievable, relevant, time-bound) included.

Strategies to use or suggest to teachers might include:
- Model responsibility.
- Incorporate cooperative learning groups into all instruction.
- Notice and name responsible actions/behaviors wherever and whenever.
- Teach, monitor and support goal setting.
- Allow choice in learning activities and demonstration of learned content.
- Use agreements for learning:
  - letters written at beginning of the year for what they hope to accomplish; reviewed at middle and end of the year
  - goal work (beyond writing goal statement)
  - planned and scheduled reflection times for personal review of progress, needs, successes
  - individually written contracts specifying desired academic behaviors

B-SMS 2. Self-discipline and self-control

Duckworth and Seligman (2005) found that "indeed, self-discipline has a bigger effect on academic performance than does intellectual talent" (p. 943) or measures of IQ.

Although often defined as synonyms, self-discipline and self-control are distinct processes. Self-control can be associated with stopping some behavior, while self-discipline can be associated with initiating a new/different way of behaving. For example, deciding to stop acting in ways that disrupt class requires self-control. Deciding to pay attention in class requires self-discipline.

"Self-control is the ability to subdue one's impulses, emotions and behaviors to achieve long-term goals" (Psychology Today, n.d.-b). It is exhibiting control when experiencing pressure for immediate urges, desires or compulsions. Self-control is the ability to delay gratification in favor of a more distant goal. It includes the ability to regulate emotions, thoughts and behaviors when tempted, refraining from immediate gratification.

Self-discipline is the ability to continue working, striving and moving forward. It is about initiating new thoughts, actions and speech. It is vital component of goal work. Self-discipline is acting in ways aligned with what you know, despite what you feel. It is making oneself do what needs to be done. Four skills are identified for self-discipline: concentration, completion, consistency and commitment (Pickhardt, 2016).

Foundational Mindsets

The mindsets foundational to this student standard include:

M 4. Self-confidence in ability to succeed

M 6. Understanding that postsecondary education and lifelong learning are necessary for long-term success

Student Learning Objective Statements

You may choose to copy one of the objectives below, modify to meet your plan more specifically, or create your own. here is also a bank of learning objectives available in the ASCA Student Standards learning objectives database.

This list of learning objectives is not exhaustive nor are the objectives listed in any special order. These are examples of student learning objectives linked to this standard. A few of the statements below offer options for refining the focus within the statement. The school counselor should select or define the appropriate focus when incorporating one of those statements.

Consider the context in which this information will be delivered to students as that may impact the selection or creation of the learning objective. The setting can both enhance and limit certain activities and strategies. Knowing if this will be delivered via small group, classroom, or large group settings may guide the decision. In addition, the primary focus of the work, wheth er academic, career or social/emotional, aids in the selection/creation process. The primary domain in which the student standard is being addressed may help refine the objective.

Students will:
- Calculate personal progress toward goals weekly.
- Compile the steps of effective goal-setting process.
- Construct a plan that divides large projects or goals into manageable steps.
- Demonstrate respectful language in uncomfortable or challenging situations.
- Describe how effort and behavior affect outcomes.
- Design a plan for small, personal rewards/celebrations to recognize positive progress.
- Employ self-calming strategies.
- Explain academic problems (missing knowledge/skills, temptations, distractions, moods, behaviors, low effort, etc.).
- Explain the reasons for school rules.
- Identify common problems encountered by students in their age group/grade level (anxiety, emotional dysregulation, worries, fears, relationship concerns, etc.).
- Identify feelings in self and others.
- Implement strategies for navigating identified barriers to academic success.
- Interpret physiological responses associated with escalating emotions.
- Label personal distractions that impede progress or school task completion.
- Manage emotions in challenging situations or when experiencing pressure.
- Name personal accomplishments, talents, special skills.
- Perform within stated classroom (or school) norms and expectations.

- Persist through tasks until completed.
- Predict strategies that might work best for them.
- Present constructive reactions when confronted with a challenging event.
- Recall specific ways in which they evidence personal improvement.
- Recall strategies for maintaining calm (self-soothing).
- Recognize personal beliefs, thoughts, communications and behaviors that escalate/de-escalate challenging events.
- Recognize when concentration or focus is waning and make necessary adjustments.
- Set, plan and work toward goals.
- State classroom norms and expectations for specified teacher(s).
- State the rules and consequences of school.
- Stop a specific behavior (noncompliance, disruption, daydreaming, etc.) when requested.
- Summarize the relationship between beliefs, thoughts, communication, behaviors and outcomes.
- Sustain attention despite disinterest, distractions or competing attractions.

Strategies to use or suggest to teachers might include:
- Provide instruction on the differences between and functions of self-discipline and self-control.
- Engage in goal work with students.
- Encourage students in taking smaller steps. Many students tend to identify and attempt major changes or giant leaps to accomplish overoptimistic goals. Instruct and support the more effective strategy of implementing smaller, easier steps that grow into appropriate habits to generate significant change. For example, initially, commit to walking one block; then, gradually increase the distance until the goal of a marathon is possible.
- Teach students to recognize and celebrate even small successes. Those small successes become more impactful in time.
- Change students' language. "I can't" becomes "I choose not to." Encourage students to move from focusing on what others did (they) to their own actions (I).
- Help students identify and prepare for potential barriers. Predict the possible problems one might encounter when attempting to change and develop a strategy for it. Use if/then charts is effective for this process.

B-SMS 3. Independent work
Developing the strategies to work independently helps students build the necessary skills of completing work on their own, managing their time and materials, and responding to challenges as they develop. It also facilitates the students' opportunities to learn how to learn, a necessary skill for lifelong learning.

Each teacher might have slightly different expectations and rules for independent work in the classroom. Students need to work on being aware of and respecting those differences. Independent work beyond the classroom typically focuses on quality completion and authentic work.

Students must develop and maintain personal motivation to do the work and do it well. In addition, there is an expectation that the completed work used resources and support appropriately, without too much reliance on others for the content, quality or completion.

Foundational Mindsets

The mindsets foundational to this student standard include:

M 3. Positive attitude toward work and learning

M 4. Self-confidence in ability to succeed

M 5. Belief in using abilities to their fullest to achieve high-quality results and outcomes

M 6. Understanding that postsecondary education and lifelong learning are necessary for long-term success

Student Learning Objective Statements

You may choose to copy one of the objectives below, modify to meet your plan more specifically, or create your own. here is also a bank of objectives available in the ASCA Student Standards learning objectives database.

This list of learning objectives is not exhaustive nor are the objectives listed in any special order. These are examples of student learning objectives that are linked to this standard. A few of the statements below offer options for refining the focus within the statement. The school counselor should select or define the appropriate focus when incorporating one of those statements.

Consider the context in which this information will be delivered to students as that may impact the selection or creation of the learning objective. The setting can both enhance and limit certain activities and strategies. Knowing if this will be delivered via small group, classroom, or large group settings may guide the decision. In addition, the primary focus of the work, whether academic, career or social/emotional, aids in the selection/creation process. The primary domain in which the student standard is being addressed may help refine the objective.

Students will:

- Balance independence with need for support.
- Calculate what speed of task completion is warranted.
- Classify tasks that require additional time.
- Complete school assignments and tasks independently.
- Compose ways in which they can connect personal interests, goals, future possibilities to course content.
- Confront challenging tasks with increased effort and motivation.
- Craft a plan, including when, where and how to ensure task completion
- Demonstrate preparedness by having all necessary tools, materials and assignments for class.
- Describe the learning process.
- Differentiate varying expectations of teachers regarding work completion, submission and quality.
- Distinguish when to set a mastery or performance goal.
- Engage in independent work and learning experiences.
- Establish a personal system for maintaining one's own motivation.
- Examine strategies to refocus when off task.
- Explain the difference between mastery and performance goals.
- Explain the role of mistakes in the learning process.

- Give examples of problems associated with perfectionism.
- Identify specific ways in which they contribute to the learning community.
- Illustrate what independent work looks like, sounds like and feels like (no electronics, heads up, focused on work/task, having something else to work on when required work completed, hands up for questions, no or brief low talking, limited quiet movement around the classroom, individuals focused on own task/work, no loud sounds, etc.).
- Initiate school assignments with minimal adult prompting.
- Integrate corrective feedback into class assignments.
- Locate academic resources and how to access them.
- Manage mistakes, setbacks and imperfect performances.
- Name and claim personal skills and talents.
- Persist when mistakes occur, working until task is completed.
- Predict how much time is needed for task completion.
- Self-monitor personal focus on assigned tasks.
- State own strengths and growing areas.
- Sustain effort to complete school assignments and tasks.
- Sustain independent work for ____ minutes.

Strategies to use or suggest to teachers might include:
- Provide instruction on what independent work looks like and sounds like. Describe the purpose, benefits, and challenges of independent work.
- Teach students how to cultivate interest in required content. Independent work is more easily accomplished when one has found a way to be interested in it.
- Teach students specific ways to self-monitor their work. Strategies might include:
  - recognizing when thoughts are interfering
  - employing thought-stopping techniques
  - building awareness of when they have ceased to work
  - learning to return to it quickly
- Buddy systems or signals from others may support self-monitoring practice.

B-SMS 4. Delayed gratification for long-term rewards

Bredehoft (2019) used the terms "patient postpone" and "instant gratifier" to convey the differences between those who could delay and not delay gratification. The article states that children learn to delay gratification when they experience three things:
1. Set attainable goals
2. Witness powerful role models delaying gratification
3. Get encouragement for delaying those rewards

The same principles apply to the school environment. Goal work, a significant and powerful skill set for students, sets up the process and experience of delaying gratification. Adults in the school can model and narrate their thinking processes around delaying immediate wants. They establish systems that allow students to practice delaying gratification, enabling vicarious and explicit learning. Finally, providing encouragement not only supports the students in the process, but it also reveals the skill as valued by adults. All work together to help students learn to delay immediate gratification for long-term rewards.

Foundational Mindsets

The mindsets foundational to this student standard include:

M 3. Positive attitude toward work and learning.

M 5. Belief in using abilities to their fullest to achieve high-quality results and outcomes.

M 6. Understanding that postsecondary education and lifelong learning are necessary for long-term success.

Student Learning Objective Statements

You may choose to copy one of the objectives below, modify to meet your plan more specifically, or create your own. here is also a bank of learning objectives available in the ASCA Student Standards the learning objectives database.

This list of learning objectives is not exhaustive nor are the objectives listed in any special order. These are examples of student learning objectives linked to this standard. A few of the statements below offer options for refining the focus within the statement. The school counselor should select or define the appropriate focus when incorporating one of those statements.

Consider the context in which this information will be delivered to students as that may impact the selection or creation of the learning objective. The setting can both enhance and limit certain activities and strategies. Knowing if this will be delivered via small group, classroom, or large group settings may guide the decision. In addition, the primary focus of the work, whether academic, career or social/emotional, aids in the selection/creation process. The primary domain in which the student standard is being addressed may help refine the objective.

Students will:
- Articulate what was learned from the experience of an unachieved goal.
- Assemble various methods to resist distractions and temptations that prolong class task completion.
- Categorize common task avoidance strategies/techniques.
- Celebrate when goals are reached.
- Clarify the reasons for persisting through challenges.
- Create a schedule for intermediary personal reinforcers for a specific goal or task completion.
- Create a specific schedule for work on a long-term project, assignment or goal.
- Demonstrate refusal strategies.
- Describe the benefits of learning and mastering skills and/or content.
- Develop and implement if/then plans for task completion.
- Engage in positive self-talk.
- Establish a positive monitoring system for movement toward goal.
- Establish intermediate goals.
- Give examples of strategies for waiting.
- Identify personal, educational, vocational, work and lifestyle preferences.
- Identify potential barriers to task completion.
- Identify strategies to eliminate automatic negative talk.
- Initiate the stated task within two minutes of request.

- Make a conscious decision to delay gratification.
- Name benefits of school assignments.
- Practice the "Seinfield strategy" (red X marked each day of positive work to create a chain of work).
- Prioritize tasks and complete the important ones first.
- Separate large or long-term assignments into manageable pieces.
- Write a long-range goal and the steps necessary to achieve it.
- Write a short-term goal and plan for school task completion.

Strategies to use or suggest to teachers might include:
- Teach students to create well-crafted goals and plans for achieving them.
- Model the delay of immediate rewards and talk out loud about one's thoughts, wishes and ultimate ability to wait.
- Teach students to use distractions when faced with a temptation or urge (count backward, do something else, move to another space/place, direct attention to a new focus, take a brief break, etc.).
- Teach students to use if/then charts to fully explore the potential benefits/costs of immediate vs. delayed gratification.

B-SMS 5. Perseverance to achieve long- and short-term goals

Research supports goal work as an important skill for school and life. Goal work has a strong impact on student achievement and student academic growth beyond the delivered intervention (Travers et al., 2014). Goal setting also has the benefits of providing students with clear directions and outcomes, which facilitates a focus on what is important. Goals create a sense of control over the future, as defined actions generate specific outcomes. They contribute to motivation, personal satisfaction and mental health. Setting goals can generate new behaviors, strengthen your focus and promote a sense of self-mastery and self-efficacy (Price-Mitchell, 2018).

There are two main goal categories:
- Mastery goals, which focus on accomplishing or mastering something
- Performance goals, which focuses on doing something better than others

Five goal-setting principles have been identified:
1. Clarity
2. Challenge
3. Commitment
4. Feedback
5. Task complexity

Achieving goals requires:
- Know your why. This is the basis for your motivation to continue striving. Why does the goal matter to you? What makes it important?
- Put the goal in writing and make it specific. Move beyond vague or undefined terms. Rather than "doing my best," identify the specific actions/behaviors that will reveal your best work.

- Imagine how realizing your stated goal will affect your life. This helps you identify the benefits and keeps you striving for success.
- Create a plan that can be scheduled and implemented. Be sure this plan is based on specific actions you can undertake rather than vague concepts.
- Identify the barriers, obstacles or problems you might encounter as you work toward realization of your stated goal. Knowing the problems before they happen gives you time to think about and plan for what to do.
- Know that achieving one goal means it is time to set another. Goal setting is an important part of life success.

Consider this process:

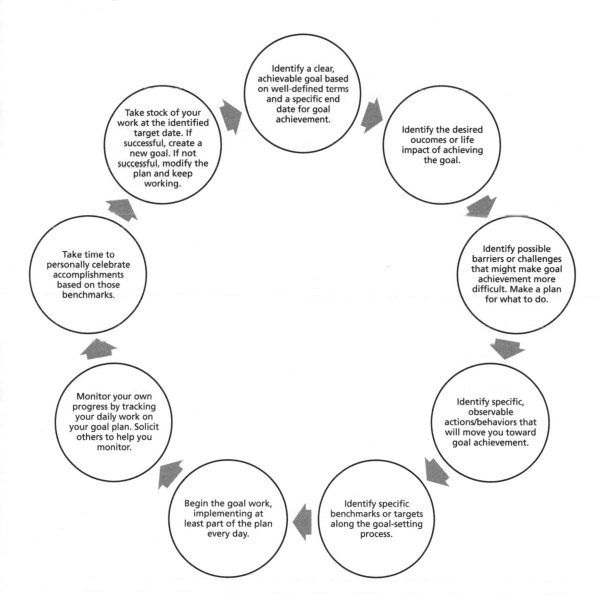

Foundational Mindsets

The mindsets foundational to this student standard include:

M 1. Belief in development of whole self, including a healthy balance of mental, social/emotional, and physical well-being

M 3. Positive attitude toward work and learning

M 5. Belief in using abilities to their fullest to achieve high-quality results and outcomes

M 6. Understanding that postsecondary education and lifelong learning are necessary for long-term success

Student Learning Objective Statements

You may choose to copy one of the objectives below, modify to meet your plan more specifically, or create your own. There is also a bank of learning objectives available in the ASCA Student Standards learning objectives database.

This list of learning objectives is not exhaustive nor are the objectives listed in any special order. These are examples of student learning objectives linked to this standard. A few of the statements below offer options for refining the focus within the statement. The school counselor should select or define the appropriate focus when incorporating one of those statements.

Consider the context in which this information will be delivered to students, as that may affect learning objective selection or creation. The setting can both enhance and limit certain activities and strategies. Knowing if this will be delivered via small group, classroom or large-group settings may guide the decision. In addition, the primary focus of the work, whether academic, career or social/emotional, aids in the selection/creation process. The primary domain in which the student standard is being addressed may help refine the objective.

Students will:
- Articulate the benefits of goal work.
- Clarify specific and clearly stated outcomes as the goal.
- Construct intermediary success points within long-term goal work.
- Compose personal goals that correspond to personal needs/wants.
- Create a vision board including commonly identified components based on a specific goal.
- Create personal affirmations that maintain motivation for goal work.
- Create personal reminders for maintaining goal focus.
- Define the actions necessary to achieve a stated goal.
- Describe the personal impact on one's life once the goal is reached.
- Determine resources that may support the goal work.
- Employ a variety of strategies when faced with barriers or mistakes during the goal work.
- Establish a support network of individuals who assist with maintaining focus on the ultimate goal.
- Establish specific directions for what to do each day to move toward goal achievement.
- Explain the value of the process of goal work.
- Give examples of the benefits goal work may have on school experience, educational outcomes and life.

- Label successive approximations and/or smaller mastery points that demonstrate movement toward goal completion.
- Measure and analyze personal goal progress, adjusting the plan as needed.
- Monitor goal progress, celebrating successful completion of identified milestones.
- Monitor self-talk.
- Name the components of an effective goal statement (SMART) and goal plan.
- Schedule periodic goal checks with a goal supporter.
- State why they feel the goal is important.
- Track goal progress daily/weekly.
- Write a goal statement, include all important components (SMART).
- Write a plan, including observable behaviors, to achieve a goal.

Strategies to use or suggest to teachers might include:
- Provide explicit instruction for creating clear, specific goals with specific, observable steps that move toward goal realization and connection to measurable outcomes. A process for self-monitoring, with intermediary success opportunities, is also critical to this instruction.
- Establish routines for individual or group monitoring of goal work for targeted students. It is especially important to make this simple and accessible for everyone. If too complex or interruptive, it is more likely to be abandoned.
- Allow time for the goal work to happen. Support the students over a semester or school year while monitoring and encouraging the goal work.
- Help students create concrete methods for checking their own goal work, clearly identifying actions or time spent on goal each week.
- Encourage middle and high school students to record goals in a personal journal in eight or more areas: academics, social life, sports and exercise, healthy eating, family and community, hobbies and interests, screen time and long-term plans. Provide support on the creation of the goals and goal plans. Revisit the journaled goals at specific times across the school year (Elias, 2019).
- Facilitate the creation of individual vision boards based on identified goals.

B-SMS 6. Ability to overcome barriers to learning
Many students encounter barriers to learning, and those barriers are as different and unique as the students themselves. It can be daunting to attempt development of specific strategies for specific barriers. Rather, we need to focus on helping students learn a process for what to do when barriers develop. We can help them channel personal resources to combat the unique constellation of problems.

There are countless barriers to learning that might affect students, including:
- Emotional barriers: fear, shame, emotional sensitivity, adjusting to change, peer pressure, fear of failure, lack of self-efficacy
- Health barriers: chronic illness, substance abuse, poor or limited nutrition, lack of access to health care, lack of sleep or interrupted sleep
- Motivational barriers: challenge that is too high or too low, lack of goals, procrastination, learning environment, lack of purpose, disengagement
- Environmental barriers: course format, teacher-student relationship, course content, physical plant, access to resources, distractions (noise, visual, disruptions, etc.)

- Social/cultural barriers: lack of community in the classroom, inability to socially interact with peers, large class size, no sense of belonging, sense of isolation, negative peer pressure
- Personal barriers: depression and other mental health concerns, poor health, dyscalculia, dyslexia, dysgraphia, language
- Other barriers: lack of focus, negative past experiences, limiting mindsets, feeling of isolation, student availability to learn or motivation, personal issues

Foundational Mindsets
The mindsets foundational to this student standard include:
M 3. Positive attitude toward work and learning
M 4. Self-confidence in ability to succeed

Student Learning Objective Statements
You may choose to copy one of the objectives below, modify to meet your plan more specifically, or create your own. There is also a bank of learning objectives available in the ASCA Student Standards learning objectives database.

This list of learning objectives is not exhaustive, nor are the objectives listed in any special order. These are examples of student learning objectives that are linked to this standard. A few of the statements below offer options for refining the focus within the statement. The school counselor should select or define the appropriate focus when incorporating one of those statements.

Consider the context in which this information will be delivered to students, as that may affect learning objective selection or creation. The setting can both enhance and limit certain activities and strategies. Knowing if this will be delivered via small-group, classroom or large-group settings may guide the decision. In addition, the primary focus of the work, whether academic, career or social/emotional, aids in the selection/creation process. The primary domain in which the student standard is being addressed may help refine the objective.

Students will:
- Analyze personal academic performance weekly and identify successes and needs.
- Articulate personal beliefs about their own efficacy (capacity, ability, skills, etc.).
- Clarify teacher expectations and discern which expectations may be personally challenging.
- Classify personal barriers that are and are not within their control.
- Create a system to track personal progress for academic work in all classes.
- Determine when help is needed.
- Define relationship between approximations and ultimate success.
- Employ identified strategies to overcome barriers.
- Establish a plan for maintaining effort and motivation when course is challenging (or uninteresting, uncomfortable, less valued, etc.).
- Examine personal feelings about school expectations and one's capacity to manage them.
- Explain how to access learning support.
- Explain the power of yet.

- Foster a positive and supportive relationship with teacher.
- Give examples of how struggles strengthen the learning process.
- Identify peers who will support positive academic efforts.
- Identify when, how and from whom to seek help.
- Illustrate the benefits of a growth mindset.
- Initiate a variety of practiced strategies to address identified barriers.
- List specific class behaviors employed by successful learners.
- Locate resources available to support learning.
- Make a plan for healthy habits (sleep/rest, nutrition and physical activity) within personal circumstances.
- Name personal barriers impeding personal learning progress.
- Record notes on positive effort and work each day.
- Relate a personal story of a negative experience in school and how it may be affecting current struggles.
- Summarize how effort affects knowledge and skills.

Strategies to use or suggest to teachers might include:
- Foster a belief in students that overcoming barriers is possible. Students need to believe in personal capacity to effect change on whatever obstacles develop.
- Foster a growth mindset.
- Use enabling language: I cannot do this yet.
- Teach students ways to build relationships (teacher to student, student to student).
- Teach students how to engage in classroom lessons appropriately and effectively.
- Assume a positive psychology/assets approach. Focus on what is right rather than what is wrong with students.
- Teach students to identify which barriers are in their control.

B-SMS 7. Effective coping skills
Coping is the use of cognitive and behavioral strategies to manage the demands of a situation (American Psychological Association, n.d.). It is not an innate skill; rather, it must be taught. Coping skills may facilitate an individual's ability to tolerate, minimize or manage some stressor. There are both positive and negative ways to address problems encountered. Effective coping skills enable one to reduce the negative feelings associated with the problem or eliminate the problem.

Psychology Today says that coping skills enable people to make sense of their negative experiences. In addition, coping skills can be learned, improved, or replaced, as needed (Scharff, 2016).

Developing coping skills includes the ability to discern the type of skill needed based on the problem presented. Problem-based coping targets the problem itself, to eliminate or change it. Emotion-based coping focuses on one's feelings associated with the problem and is used when the problem is beyond the individual's control or the individual does not want to change the problem. Emotion-based coping is not about removing or avoiding feelings; rather, it is about finding healthier ways to experience or express them, ways to self-soothe, distract or tolerate those feelings.

Coping skills may also be proactive. For example, avoiding places, people or situations associated with the stressor/problem reduces the likelihood of encountering the problem. When it cannot be avoided, proactive coping includes knowing/rehearsing a variety of strategies to employ to manage the problem.

Foundational Mindsets

The mindsets foundational to this student standard include:

M 3. Positive attitude toward work and learning

M 4. Self-confidence in ability to succeed

Student Learning Objective Statements

You may choose to copy one of the objectives below, modify to meet your plan more specifically, or create your own. There is also a bank of learning objectives available in the ASCA Student Standards learning objectives database.

This list of learning objectives is not exhaustive, nor are the objectives listed in any special order. These are examples of student learning objectives that are linked to this standard. A few of the statements below offer options for refining the focus within the statement. The school counselor should select or define the appropriate focus when incorporating one of those statements.

Consider the context in which this information will be delivered to students as that may affect learning objective selection or creation. The setting can both enhance and limit certain activities and strategies. Knowing if this will be delivered via small-group, classroom or large-group settings may guide the decision. In addition, the primary focus of the work, whether academic, career or social/emotional, aids in the selection/creation process. The primary domain in which the student standard is being addressed may help refine the objective.

Students will:

- Analyze self-talk and how it affects school performance.
- Categorize possible responses for challenging situations.
- Clarify what is and is not within one's personal control.
- Classify healthy emotion-focused coping strategies.
- Compile a list of coping strategies for common social/emotional issues encountered in school.
- Define anxiety and identify relevant coping strategies.
- Demonstrate impulse control.
- Describe personal values, beliefs and challenges.
- Employ identified coping strategies to address learning barriers.
- Employ strategies to address specific social/emotional concerns.
- Engage mindfulness activities to enhance learning.
- Establish a comprehensive feelings vocabulary (identifying basic categories of feelings, learning more words, understanding how different words indicate levels of intensity).
- Give examples of personal support systems.

- Give examples of the role/function of mistakes and imperfect performance in the learning process.
- Identify common problems encountered by students in their age group/grade level (anxiety, emotional dysregulation, worries, fears, relationship concerns, etc.).
- Illustrate how feelings are commonly expressed in self and others.
- Interpret feelings and level of intensity in self and others.
- Link future outcomes to immediate responses to challenges.
- Name personal social/emotional resources and/or supports (school counselors, mentors, positive friends, etc.).
- Name personal strengths and growth needs.
- Plan access to help when needed.
- Predict something positive that might evolve from a current problem.
- Recall own resilience and strengths.
- Recognize anxious feelings and employ a coping strategy.
- Recognize feelings of frustration in specific courses and employ coping skills.
- Recognize physical reactions associated with frustration.
- Rehearse strategies to avoid places (people, situations) associated with stressors.
- Summarize mindfulness and associated strategies.
- Understand the importance of choice in generating personal coping skills.

Strategies to use or suggest to teachers might include:
- Mindfulness activities
- Deep breathing techniques (pinwheel, bubbles, flower/candle, etc.)
- Positive self-talk
- Focus on positives (list your favorite things, identify one good thing per class/day, etc.)
- Build feelings vocabulary
- Read stories/books focused on someone's effective coping
- Teach students to generate the best type of solutions to specific problems:
  - Problem-focused coping: attempt to modify the source of the problem. Examples may include:
    - Actively problem solve
    - Create a to-do list
    - Know when to walk away
    - Set boundaries (responsibilities, schedules, relationships, etc.)
    - Join/create a support network
  - Emotion-focused coping: attempt to modify the feelings/emotions the individual experiences about the problem. Examples may include:
    - Exercise, do something distracting but productive (clean, organize), engage in a hobby, spend time in nature, garden, yoga
    - Journal, draw, meditate, listen to music, color, use progressive muscle relaxation, visualize or look at photos of your preferred place
    - Generate a gratitude list (things you are grateful for)
    - Reframe one's thinking, creating personal mantras (I can do this; this, too, shall pass), listing the things that bring you joy

B-SMS 8. Balance of school, home, and community activities

Achieving optimal school performance is facilitated by the ability to balance school and life (Johns Hopkins University, n.d.). Several skills identified as associated with achieving balance include:

- Scheduling
- Creating weekly to-do lists
- Prioritizing
- Dividing large tasks/projects into smaller parts
- Setting goals and deadlines
- Avoiding perfectionism
- Assessing time wasted honestly

Foundational Mindsets

The mindsets foundational to this student standard include:

M 1. Belief in development of whole self, including a healthy balance of mental, social/ emotional, and physical well-being

M 2. Sense of acceptance, respect, support and inclusion for self and others in the school environment

M 3. Positive attitude toward work and learning

M 5. Belief in using abilities to their fullest to achieve high-quality results and outcomes

Student Learning Objective Statements

You may choose to copy one of the objectives below, modify to meet your plan more specifically, or create your own. There is also a bank of learning objectives available in the ASCA Student Standards learning objectives database.

This list of learning objectives is not exhaustive, nor are the objectives listed in any special order. These are examples of student learning objectives that are linked to this standard. A few of the statements below offer options for refining the focus within the statement. The school counselor should select or define the appropriate focus when incorporating one of those statements.

Consider the context in which this information will be delivered to students as that may affect learning objective selection or creation. The setting can both enhance and limit certain activities and strategies. Knowing if this will be delivered via small-group, class-room or large-group settings may guide the decision. In addition, the primary focus of the work, whether academic, career or social/emotional, aids in the selection/creation process. The primary domain in which the student standard is being addressed may help refine the objective.

Students will:

- Adjust personal schedules (or habits) to reduce time consumers and time wasters.
- Assess personal time usage to discover time consumers and time wasters.
- Construct a system to set priorities between competing tasks/interests/responsibilities.
- Create a balanced personal calendar incorporating healthy habits (rest/sleep, exercise, scheduled activities, study, school, leisure, etc.).

- Describe how to make good decisions around peer relationships, commitments to others, clubs, activities and family responsibilities.
- Design a process/rubric for making decisions regarding whether to become involved in various activities, events, projects, etc.
- Design flexible weekly schedules to accommodate all demands associated with school, home and other activities.
- Determine the benefits and costs of involvement in a specific project, team, club or extracurricular activity.
- Determine ways in which to reduce time demands without giving up a specific commitment.
- Develop supportive relationships with peers and adults.
- Engage in consistent goal work.
- Establish priorities for determining personal involvement and commitments.
- Evaluate life goals and what is required to realize them.
- Explain personal values/beliefs and how they might be affecting current decisions.
- Give examples of how to balance demands of school, home and community.
- Identify a personal rubric for establishing priorities.
- Identify resources and support systems that can provide help when needed.
- Organize schedules reflecting a positive balance between school, home and community.
- Participate and collaborate in discussions with diverse peers on resiliency and maintaining a healthy balance.
- Practice effective refusal skills when setting boundaries around personal commitments and responsibilities.
- Predict potential conflicts between demands of school, home and/or community.
- Report value/benefits derived from school, home and/or community.
- Seek support from adults when feeling overwhelmed by commitments or expectations.
- Solicit help in determining how to manage school, home and community expectations.
- Specify what to consider when making decisions around peer relationships, commitments to others, clubs, activities or family responsibilities.
- State reasons for limiting/refusing involvement in an event or activity.
- Summarize how community affects school, home and one's future.
- Summarize how home impacts school, community and/or one's future.
- Summarize how school affects home, community and/or one's future.
- Use weekly to-do lists

Strategies to use or suggest to teachers might include:
- Provide explicit instruction/discussion on setting boundaries and limits. This strategy includes understanding the significance and potential impact of saying yes and no to opportunities/activities.
- Explore leisure activity possibilities. Help students discover ways they can relax and have fun. These need not be huge celebrations or events. It might be taking time to read, pause, chat with friends/family, etc.
- Provide explicit instruction and practice on how to schedule effectively and why it is so important. Effective scheduling includes identifying specific times for certain things to happen while allowing enough flexibility for rescheduling when competing activities or assignments develop.

- Help students (and the adults in their lives) focus on process over product. Rather than getting perfect scores or perfect grades on every assignment or never making a mistake, help students appreciate the value of learning. Typically, those who value and work for learning mastery experience higher grades as a benefit. Understanding and operating from that perspective can reduce stress as well as increase content/skills acquired.
- Understand that "perfect is the enemy of good." Perfect should not be praised, endorsed or valued. Those who strive only for perfection often limit their activities and engagement out of a fear of missed perfection.
- Teach students to identify when they might be overwhelmed and develop strategies for reducing those feelings (go for a walk, call a friend, use breathing techniques, color, etc.).
- Teach students to use if/then planning for building good habits. This approach is about utilizing time and space that might otherwise be wasted. For example, some homework could be done in the car on the way to a sports event or practice or while waiting on a sibling. (If I am at my sister's soccer practice, I will do my math homework.) This strategy can also be facilitated by teaching students to always have some schoolwork or task with them. By doing so, they can more effectively use their time.
- Help students create/find support networks (peers, family, school) who value the student's life goals and will both support and protect their time spent on what needs to be accomplished.
- Facilitate school extracurricular participation. Joining a club, sport or organization might mean extra time and responsibilities, but when chosen well and facilitated by a school adult who understands priorities, it can become another support group as well as a motivator for maintaining school balance.
- Exercise caution and understanding when talking with students about their many commitments and responsibilities. Taking time to hear the reasons behind what they are choosing to do is important. Learn and support their values and needs, and then help them balance what they must.

B-SMS 9. Personal safety skills

Students must have personal safety skills. The world contains many opportunities for hurt, and it can seem impossible to equip each student with the precise skills needed to withstand all potential dangers.

Violence in schools continues to be prevalent, from playground bullying to physical fights in the hallways to shooters on campus. The internet offers rich opportunities for exploration and learning while also enabling cyberbullying and exploitation. The marginalization of some student groups exacerbates both their vulnerability and their experiences of being targeted. Mental health concerns continue to rise while suicide ideation and completion increase.

The skills needed to stay safe are abundant, and there are many programs available for teaching needed skills to students in the K-12 setting. School counselors can focus on a broader perspective of what it takes to stay safe. Consider these skills that contribute to student safety (NASP):
- Self-advocacy skills
- Refusal skills

- Decision-making skills
- Understanding of the "power of one"
- Creation of positive interpersonal relationship skills
- Understanding and creation of healthy personal boundaries
- Coping skills
- Self-care skills
- Building of emotional competency, including the ability to manage strong emotions

Foundational Mindsets

The mindset foundational to this student standard is:

M 1. Belief in development of whole self, including a healthy balance of mental, social/ emotional and physical well-being

Student Learning Objective Statements

You may choose to copy one of the objectives below, modify to meet your plan more specifically, or create your own. There is also a bank of learning objectives available in the ASCA Student Standards learning objectives database.

This list of learning objectives is not exhaustive nor are the objectives listed in any special order. These are examples of student learning objectives that are linked to this standard. A few of the statements below offer options for refining the focus within the statement. The school counselor should select or define the appropriate focus when incorporating one of those statements.

Consider the context in which this information will be delivered to students as that may affect learning objective selection or creation. The setting can both enhance and limit certain activities and strategies. Knowing if this will be delivered via small-group, class-room or large-group settings may guide the decision. In addition, the primary focus of the work, whether academic, career or social/emotional, aids in the selection/creation process. The primary domain in which the student standard is being addressed may help refine the objective.

Students will:
- Articulate personal boundaries (physical, social, emotional, safety, etc.).
- Communicate personal needs, fears, wants to appropriate individuals who can help.
- Create a plan to stay safe in a variety of environments and situations.
- Create positive relationships with supportive adults.
- Describe how to get help when confronted with dangerous situations or unhealthy behaviors.
- Describe multiple de-escalation techniques.
- Design a personal schedule that includes healthy physical activity, rest and nutrition within one's own circumstances.
- Devise and manage a personal plan for physical health.
- Devise and manage a personal plan for social/emotional health.
- Employ rehearsed/practiced strategies when feeling unsafe.
- Evaluate the safety of common situations and environments.
- Explain personal advocacy skills.

- Explain the absence of blame or responsibility when unsafe things happen (even if they made poor decisions).
- Formulate a personal plan for managing online bullying.
- Give examples of how to avoid risky situations and environments.
- Identify traits/characteristics of safe/unsafe environments, situations, people, places, etc.
- Illustrate a healthy decision-making model.
- Interpret personal feelings and thoughts about their safety.
- Know standard guidelines for healthy sleep/diet/exercise habits.
- Name adults available to help in different settings (class, school, home, with peers, etc.).
- Name resources and support systems.
- Recognize personal triggers linked to escalating conflict.
- Report unsafe events, circumstances, situations, people, etc.
- Understand the specific needs of their body to support physical health.
- Validate reasons and ways to say no.

Strategies to use or suggest to teachers might include:
- Ensure school counselors are in the conversation when schools and districts consider personal safety programs and curricula. This conversation needs to occur across the K–12 setting. Safety skills are needed at all ages.
- Create a culture of respect for all and sense of belonging for each.
- Teach school adults to listen appropriately and respond appropriately when students might be ready to disclose concerns.
- Instruct students on skills contributing to the ability to stay safe, as well as how to return to safety when problems occur.
- Facilitate instruction across the K–12 settings on specific programs for:
  - Emotional safety
  - Physical safety
  - Bullying
  - Cybersafety
  - Substance abuse
  - Emergency readiness

B-SMS 10. Ability to manage transitions and ability to adapt to change

Transitions occur in schools throughout the school day and across the school years. Moving from activity to activity, class to class, grade to grade and school to school all offer opportunities for growth and challenges. Ending one event, period or phase and being ready for the next event, period or phase requires multiple skills.

The daily transitions within the classroom or the school, with the associated increased sense of freedom and less direct teacher management, engender multiple opportunities for students to forget rules and expectations, be targeted by another or demonstrate significant maturity and responsibility. When approaching the big transitions in school life, moving from one grade to the next or one school to another, one must manage conflicting feelings (sadness and excitement, for example), maintain a confident sense of self (regardless of internal struggles) and demonstrate a willingness to explore new experiences, responsibilities and relationships.

Beyond the known transitions fixed across the days and years of school, unexpected changes occur, typically with little or no warning. Students need the self-management to approach and react to all these effectively.

Foundational Mindsets
The mindsets foundational to this student standard include:
M 3. Positive attitude toward work and learning
M 4. Self-confidence in ability to succeed
M 5. Belief in using abilities to their fullest to achieve high-quality results and outcomes

Student Learning Objective Statements
You may choose to copy one of the objectives below, modify to meet your plan more specifically, or create your own. There is also a bank of learning objectives available in the ASCA Student Standards learning objectives database.

This list of learning objectives is not exhaustive nor are the objectives listed in any special order. These are examples of student learning objectives that are linked to this standard. A few of the statements below offer options for refining the focus within the statement. The school counselor should select or define the appropriate focus when incorporating one of those statements.

Consider the context in which this information will be delivered to students as that may affect learning objective selection or creation. The setting can both enhance and limit certain activities and strategies. Knowing if this will be delivered via small-group, class-room or large-group settings may guide the decision. In addition, the primary focus of the work, whether academic, career or social/emotional, aids in the selection/creation process. The primary domain in which the student standard is being addressed may help refine the objective.

Students will:
- Acknowledge and name experiences of conflicting emotions that occur simultaneously.
- Define varying expectations and responsibilities across different settings, classes, instructors, etc.
- Demonstrate appropriate, healthy adaptation to transitions across settings, classes, grades, schools.
- Demonstrate expected behaviors while following adult directions and maintaining safety when unexpected changes occur.
- Describe potential benefits for change and/or transitions.
- Engage in new experiences.
- Explain importance of personal responsibility and self-management during transitions.
- Express emotions safely and respectfully while following adult directions and maintaining safety when unexpected changes occur.
- Give examples of how change is a normal part of life.
- Identify potential positives that may result from upcoming change.
- Maintain behavioral expectations during transition times.
- Manage grades after transition occurs (new class, new teacher, new school, new grade, etc.).

- Manage new responsibilities when school adjustments are made (changing study habits, adding in credit recovery, moving to more rigorous coursework, etc.)
- Name potential challenges that may occur in upcoming change.
- Name the new/different responsibilities associated with various changes.
- Practice using personal techniques to maintain sense of calm during stressful periods.
- Predict possible problems or challenging demands of new settings, class, grade, school.
- Seek to establish new, positive relationships with peers in new settings.
- Self-soothe in times of unexpected stress.
- Summarize how to build new relationships when changes occur.

Strategies to use or suggest to teachers might include:
- Explain, demonstrate and role play what effective transitions look like, sound like and feel like.
- Set clear and realistic expectations for what comes next. Clarify reality and dispel myths associated with the significant transitions. Specifically define and describe the smaller changes.
- Design and implement special activities around the big transitions (into kindergarten, into third grade, into middle school, into high school, out of high school). Deliver classroom instruction addressing common experiences, potential problems and realistic expectations. Organize field trips to new school sites or enjoyable social events to generate positive bonds and reduce anxieties. Bring in special guests, near peers, school leaders (adult and student) to talk with students about the positives associated with the next phase.
- Prepare and distribute lists of resources, special programs, clubs and activities at the new school/grade.
- Facilitate professional development for teachers/faculty on best practices for managing student transitions.

CHAPTER 5

Behavior Standards: Social Skills

Behavior standards include behaviors commonly associated with being a successful student. These are the visible, outward signs that a student is engaged and putting forth effort to learn. The behaviors are grouped into three subcategories, the third of which is social skills.

Social skills are the acceptable behaviors that improve social interactions, such as those between peers or between students and adults. There are 10 social skills standards. Students will demonstrate the following standards through classroom lessons, activities and/or individual/small-group counseling.

B-SS 1. Effective oral and written communication skills and listening skills
B-SS 2. Positive and supportive relationships with students who are like and different from them
B-SS 3. Positive relationships with adults that support success
B-SS 4. Empathy
B-SS 5. Ethical decision-making and social responsibility
B-SS 6. Effective collaboration and cooperation skills
B-SS 7. Leadership and teamwork skills to work effectively in diverse teams
B-SS 8. Advocacy skills for self and others and ability to assert self when necessary
B-SS 9. Social maturity and behaviors appropriate to the situation and environment
B-SS 10. Cultural awareness, sensitivity and responsiveness

Social skills are a necessary component to developing positive relationships, gaining access to opportunities and avoiding potentially negative consequences. They are demonstrated through commonly acceptable behaviors that improve social interactions and are considered a career-readiness skill.

Social skills enable students to work with both peers and adults and help them realize personal goals. Social skills increase students' capacity to work in groups, participate in class discussions and develop a sense of belonging. Learning is a social activity with greater understanding achieved through interactions with others.

Although no causal relationship between social skills and academic outcomes has been definitively linked, correlations are well-documented in the research literature. Social skills serve as academic enablers by facilitating engagement.

Chapter 7 Evidence on Social Skills in "Teaching Adolescents to Become Learners," one of the key sources for the development of the ASCA Student Standards, identifies several key takeaways:

- Understanding the relationship between social skills and academic performance is important.
  - The effect of social skills on academics is indirect.
  - Social skills enhance social interactions that increase learning or minimize disruptions.
- Social skills are linked to academic performance.
  - Social/emotional adjustment is predictive of achievement test scores at grades 1, 3, 6 and age 16 (Farrington et al., 2012, p. 48).
  - Social/emotional interventions have positive effects on academic achievement (Farrington et al., 2012, p. 48).
  - Positive social skills have been found to predict GPA, positively correlate to grades, predict future academic performance and may act as "academic enablers."
  - Teachers value prosocial skills and may reward good behavior with higher grades.
- The school and classroom environment has a significant impact on social skills.
  - Interpersonal, instructional and environmental contexts affect students' social behavior and academic performance.
  - Classroom structures may cause or exacerbate poor social behavior.
  - Schools and classrooms that generate more prosocial behaviors include:
    - ▶ High expectations
    - ▶ Caring teacher/student relationships
    - ▶ Engaging instructional practices
    - ▶ Safe and orderly environments
- Interventions designed to establish or promote social skills are:
  - More likely to produce change when led by well-trained professionals
  - More likely to result in enduring change when focus on behavioral skill building
  - More effective when they're schoolwide
  - More effective when they explicitly teach and model social skills and provide opportunities to practice social skills in a variety of settings

B-SS 1. Effective oral and written communication skills and listening skills

The ability to communicate effectively and appropriately is well-established as a significant part of prosocial skills. Three broad categories of communication are represented in this standard: oral communication, written communication and listening skills.

Oral communication skills include the ability to recognize and regulate paralanguage, including voice tone, voice volume, accent, pitch, speech rate, modulation and fluency; nonverbal language including facial expressions, body movement, posture, gestures, eye contact and distancing; and the actual spoken communication, including word choice, clarity of expression, simplicity of messaging and adjustment of responses. In addition to all of these, listening skills, emotional regulation and being able to participate respectfully in the give and take required in most communication exchanges are essential.

Written communication skills focus on the ability to communicate clearly and concisely in writing. Five elements of quality writing are often cited: clarity, conciseness, tone, active voice, and grammar/punctuation. Clarity ensures the audience understands the message. It is developed through simple language and a focus on specific information. Conciseness requires efficiency and limits on what information is included – only that which is necessary. Tone refers to the overall feeling of the writing and can vary depending on the intended audience. Professional writings require professional tones with more formality, including structure and word choice. Active voice creates sentences that flow better and allow for quicker reading. It is more accessible and easier to follow. Grammar and punctuation address the correct use of commas, articles, prepositions, verb tense and all other basic grammar rules. The skill with which the rules of writing are employed either enhances or detracts from the message.

Effective listening is the ability to receive and interpret messages. Different types of listening are utilized based on what the listener is trying to achieve. We listen for enjoyment, to obtain information, to understand or to learn.

Appreciative listening occurs when you are listening for enjoyment. It tends to occur naturally when listening by choice to music, speeches, entertainment, etc. Empathic listening provides evidence of a caring, concerned listener. This occurs when one is trying to understand another person or situation. It requires being fully present, listening mindfully and maintaining a focus on the speaker. Comprehensive listening occurs when trying to gather information, whether a news report, directions for completing a task or getting to a destination, a class lecture on something that needs to be learned and remembered. Finally, critical listening involves focused listening with integrated comparisons, analysis and evaluation to all parts of the message. Critical listening involves critical thinking.

Listening skills are specific techniques employed by effective listeners. They may include paying attention, demonstrating that one is listening, offering feedback, deferring judgment and responding appropriately. Active listening is a teachable skill that trains an individual to fully concentrate, utilizing all senses.

Foundational Mindsets
The mindsets foundational to this student standard include:
M 1. Belief in development of whole self, including a healthy balance of mental, social/emotional, and physical well-being
M 4. Self-confidence in ability to succeed

Student Learning Objective Statements
You may choose to copy one of the objectives below, modify to meet your plan more specifically or create your own. There is also a bank of learning objectives in the ASCA Student Standards learning objectives database.

This list of learning objectives is not exhaustive nor are the objectives listed in any special order. These are examples of student learning objectives that are linked to this standard. A few of the statements below offer options for refining the focus within the statement. The school counselor should select or define the appropriate focus when incorporating one of those statements.

Consider the context in which this information will be delivered to students as that may affect learning objective selection or creation. The setting can both enhance and limit certain activities and strategies. Knowing if this will be delivered via small-group, classroom or large-group settings may guide the decision. In addition, the primary focus of the work, whether academic, career or social/emotional, aids in the selection/creation process. The primary domain in which the student standard is being addressed may help refine the objective.

Students will:
■ Adhere to agreed-upon rules for discussions when resolving conflicts with peers (e.g., gaining the floor in respectful ways, listening to others with care, speaking one at a time about the topics and texts under discussion).
■ Apply self-soothing/self-calming strategies when communicating with others.
■ Define persuasive essay.
■ Demonstrate listening skills.
■ Demonstrate respectful oral communication (voice tone, volume, word choice, etc.).
■ Differentiate when to ask questions effectively.
■ Disengage from escalating conversations, discussions or debates.
■ Explain etiquette rules for online communication.
■ Explain how negative words can hurt others.
■ Express personal thoughts, opinions and/or feelings to others.
■ Give examples of how to end or leave a discussion without generating escalating emotions.
■ Illustrate respectful body posture to facilitate conversation and discussion.
■ Interpret language, paralanguage and body language.
■ Itemize the specific steps of effective test preparation.
■ List common mistakes in email exchanges.
■ List problematic body posture that may discourage conversation and discussion.
■ Model active listening skills.
■ Monitor and name personal feelings when communicating with others.
■ Paraphrase another student's or a teacher's ideas, thoughts or opinions succinctly and accurately.
■ Produce a clear and coherent college application essay, highlighting personal achievements and demonstrating creativity.
■ Provide authentic, respectful feedback during discussions and conversations.
■ Provide details on how to ask questions effectively.
■ Recognize when ending or leaving a discussion is necessary.
■ Script the necessary steps for tracking school assignments.
■ Speak audibly and clearly to express thoughts, feelings and ideas during conflicts.
■ State the procedures/rules for typing and formatting an email.
■ Structure a respectful argument for a personal position/opinion.

- Summarize guidelines for listening.
- Write a letter to a school counselor (teacher, employer, etc.) requesting a reference, recommendation or referral.
- Write persuasive letters, personal statements, application essays.

Effective strategies to use or suggest to teachers might include:

Oral Communication Skills
- Incorporate role-play opportunities for students in lessons and groups.
- Promote or sponsor various leadership groups and/or experiences in the school setting that include opportunities for public speaking, debate or polite conversations. For example, high schools might conduct special events like interview day, networking receptions, formal meal, etc. to help students develop skills and behaviors needed to effectively interact in the working world. Middle schools might offer debate or public speaking clubs. Elementary schools might create a board games club that allows students to practice speaking and sharing in a social/entertaining setting.
- Incorporate opportunities for students to present findings, opinions, thoughts orally in classroom and group settings. Explicitly state expectations for both the speaker and listener, and reinforce those who meet those expectations. Cooperative learning groups often include a brief oral presentation regarding the work accomplished by the group.

Written Communication Skills
- Collaborate with English departments to facilitate the development of writing skills associated with social skills, especially around respectful persuasion and/or writing as part of life. For example, school counselors and writing teachers in a high school may collaborate to help students write their personal statements required for many postsecondary options. A similar collaboration might occur in the elementary setting as students write letters to next year's teacher and explain their hopes/needs/expectations.
- Incorporate a journal into classroom instruction. Students may respond to an essential question or a specific prompt linked to the lesson. Depending on caseload size, school counselors may or may not attempt to respond to journal writings. Regardless, the journal entries serve as both an opportunity to write and a time of reflections necessary for meaningful learning.
- Incorporate letter writing into classroom instruction. Students may write letters to school administrators, letters to political or government individuals or agencies, letters to the editor seeking to make a change or explain what needs students value. Again, collaborating with classroom teachers is helpful.

Effective Listening
- Explicitly teach specific skills associated with effective listening:
  - Face the speaker and maintain eye contact
  - Be attentive, but relaxed
  - Keep an open mind
  - Listen to the words and try to picture what is being said
  - Do not interrupt or try to impose your own solutions
  - Wait for the speaker to pause, and then ask clarifying questions
  - Ask questions only to ensure understanding
  - Try to feel what the speaker is feeling

- Provide regular feedback (affirmations, natural reactions, nods, etc.)
- Pay attention to the nonverbal cues
- Teach active listening skills.
  - Give the speaker your undivided attention and acknowledge the message
  - Show you are listening (face the speaker, make eye contact, lean in slightly, relax your body to a position of openness, nod, etc.)
  - Reflect or paraphrase
  - Provide respectful feedback
  - Validate feelings
  - Avoid interrupting
  - Defer judgment
  - Don't give advice
  - Ask thoughtful questions
  - Respond appropriately
- Conduct listening exercises:
  - Students work in pairs in which one student tells a short story about an event, information about something or any directed conversation. The listener then tries to summarize and paraphrase what was said. Have students change roles and repeat, repeat, repeat.
  - Identify some specific keywords, phrases or markers students should listen for during a reading. Someone in the group then reads a predetermined selection. Listeners may simply count/tally the number of times the keyword was used, make note of how the keyword was used each time or follow some practiced response each time it is heard. For example, one might read a short version of a child's story and give directions to different groups of students to do something when a repeated key phrase is uttered (e.g., stand up and blow air through your mouth whenever the "wolf huffs and puffs").

B-SS 2. Positive, respectful and supportive relationships with students who are similar to and different from them

Positive and supportive relationships with peers is an essential factor in believing one belongs in a group, class or school. Furthermore, that sense of belonging is foundational to learning. Therefore, it is essential that schools establish a climate in which all students believe they have a place and that opportunities for creating positive relationships are pervasive and prevalent. Lonely, isolated, neglected or rejected students are less likely to feel connected, fully engage or effectively learn. School counselors are essential to building that culture of inclusion and creating those opportunities.

Supporting the development of positive and supportive peer relationships requires schools to provide explicit instruction on social skills, understand and promote social/emotional learning and incorporate specific experiences/activities that build peer friendships. In addition, a positive culture on the playground must be studied, implemented, monitored and supported. Quality friendships provide companionship, validation, support and connections.

Supporting positive and supportive peer relationships might include:

- Creating opportunities for students to have conversations.
- Ensuring adults in the building are positive role models for respecting others, caring about others, engaging in appropriate conversations, etc.
- Promoting opportunities for students to explore common interests.
- Using peer and near-peer tutoring and mentoring programs.
- Exploring technology and media for additional resources.
- Offering professional development for teachers on how to build community in the classroom.
- Avoiding using loss of certain social privileges as a disciplinary response. For example, "silent lunch" or loss of recess might be a common response in the elementary setting; however, these are the times when students might engage in relationship building. Those who tend to lose these activities might be the ones who need them the most.

Foundational Mindsets
The mindsets foundational to this student standard include:

M 2. Sense of acceptance, respect, support and inclusion for self and others in the school environment

M 3. Positive attitude toward work and learning

M 5. Belief in using abilities to their fullest to achieve high-quality results and outcomes

Student Learning Objective Statements
You may choose to copy one of the objectives below, modify to meet your plan more specifically, or create your own. There is also a bank of learning objectives in the ASCA Student Standards learning objectives database.

This list of learning objectives is not exhaustive nor are the objectives listed in any special order. These are examples of student learning objectives that are linked to this standard. A few of the statements below offer options for refining the focus within the statement. The school counselor should select or define the appropriate focus when incorporating one of those statements.

Consider the context in which this information will be delivered to students as that may affect learning objective selection or creation. The setting can both enhance and limit certain activities and strategies. Knowing if this will be delivered via small-group, classroom or large-group settings may guide the decision. In addition, the primary focus of the work, whether academic, career or social/emotional, aids in the selection/creation process. The primary domain in which the student standard is being addressed may help refine the objective.

Students will:

- Accept compliments.
- Ascertain personal skills and interests.
- Characterize influence of peer relationships.
- Clarify process, roles and function of friendship.
- Create and sustain positive social relationships.
- Demonstrate active listening skills.

- Demonstrate conflict resolution skills.
- Distinguish between positive friendships promoting growth and helpful habits and negative friendships limiting or negatively influencing growth and helpful habits.
- Engage in a range of conversations and collaborations with diverse partners to understand different cultures and how they contribute to the school community.
- Exhibit communication skills with peers.
- Explain how word choice and tone can foster misunderstanding and conflict.
- Express emotions during social interactions in ways that foster equanimity.
- Follow agreed-upon rules for problem solving (e.g., talking it out, walking away, making a deal).
- Give compliments.
- Give examples of how to develop and maintain a positive mindset.
- Identify real-life connections between friendly and helpful people to create positive and supportive relationships with other students.
- Identify school opportunities for building positive relationships with students (or adults).
- Illustrate peer influences/pressure.
- Infer how interests and skills might lead to connections with other students.
- Initiate, sustain and end conversations respectfully with peers.
- List the skills needed to make friends.
- List personally preferred traits/qualities of a good friend.
- Name common/expected social mores and manners.
- Negotiate and resolve conflicts with friends.
- Participate in relevant student groups or extracurricular activities, based on personal skills, talents and interests.
- Recognize and interpret verbal and nonverbal social cues.
- Seek support when needed.
- Share materials, time, attention and choice with others.
- State own preferences for social interactions and relationships, including time spent (alone and/or with others) and the types of interactions (group size, content, location, timing, etc.).
- Summarize how to maintain positive relationships.

Effective strategies to use or suggest to teachers might include:
- Cooperative learning activities in the classroom facilitate social skills building. Incorporating this instructional strategy in any lesson offers opportunities for students to practice their social skills.
- Ask students to identify and describe the traits and behaviors of students they believe have effective social skills. Brainstorm the list, and then discuss items on the list, defining and offering examples for each. Depending on the setting and students, consider discussing which represent strengths and growing opportunities for students.
- New student groups may include the new student and a student ambassador who helps the new person integrate more easily into the school environment. Build in social activities.
- Conduct small-group counseling experiences facilitating the growth of positive peer relationships and prosocial skills.

- Add peer tutor programs involving a slightly older or more-skilled student to work with younger/less-skilled students. Students who are selected as peer tutors must be trained and periodically re-briefed. The program should be well-monitored.
- Participate in the annual "Mix it Up at Lunch Day."
- Conduct book studies (with students and/or faculty) focusing on positive peer relationships.
- Advocate for special schoolwide events focused on social interactions:
  - Game time: various board games and group games offered with students self-selecting or receiving a set of tickets for specific game areas
  - Invention time: small groups of students receive a packet of materials, each getting the same supplies, and have a predetermined period to create something
  - Building time: like invention time, but groups may focus on specific building supplies (Lego, Tinker Toys, wooden blocks, erector sets, etc.)
  - Interest groups: Seek adult sponsors for establishing clubs around specific areas of interest students can enroll in and explore (STEM, art, music, dance, writing, reading, etc.)

B-SS 3. Positive relationships with adults to support success

Research consistently identifies the importance of a caring adult in the school for students to succeed. Students who perceive a positive relationship with a teacher are more engaged, motivated and prosocial, which enables improved behavior and achievement.

These relationships matter at every age. Greater Good in Education (n.d.) cites the research:
- Relationships with teachers in preschool and kindergarten that are emotionally supportive and less conflictual enable social and academic competence in students.
- Positive relationships with teacher in elementary and middle school are associated with greater student engagement and improved social and behavioral outcomes.
- High school students who are positively connected with their teachers are less likely to engage in risky behaviors.

Research supports the importance of students having positive relationships with adults. Therefore, teachers, faculty and staff must always work toward creating positive relationships with students. Defining that positive relationship between adults and students may include:
- Is close and supportive but not overly dependent
- Is honest and open, with the adult offering thoughtful feedback
- Sets and maintains boundaries and high expectations
- Is respectful of and values the other
- Offers second chances
- Provides challenge with appropriate support

Foundational Mindsets
The mindsets foundational to this student standard include:
M 2. Sense of acceptance, respect, support and inclusion for self and others in the school environment
M 3. Positive attitude toward work and learning

Student Learning Objective Statements

You may choose to copy one of the objectives below, modify to meet your plan more specifically, or create your own. There is also a bank of learning objectives available in the ASCA Student Standards learning objectives database.

This list of learning objectives is not exhaustive nor are the objectives listed in any special order. These are examples of student learning objectives that are linked to this standard. A few of the statements below offer options for refining the focus within the statement. The school counselor should select or define the appropriate focus when incorporating one of those statements.

Consider the context in which this information will be delivered to students as that may affect learning objective selection or creation. The setting can both enhance and limit certain activities and strategies. Knowing if this will be delivered via small-group, classroom or large-group settings may guide the decision. In addition, the primary focus of the work, whether academic, career or social/emotional, aids in the selection/creation process. The primary domain in which the student standard is being addressed may help refine the objective.

Students will:
- Accept corrective feedback.
- Acknowledge others' values.
- Advocate for own needs.
- Classify behaviors as within or outside of healthy boundaries.
- Defend an opinion following rules of healthy debate.
- Define parameters and behaviors for engaging with adults.
- Demonstrate respectful communication skills with adults.
- Determine the best times to seek help from a teacher.
- Engage with supportive adults within established boundaries.
- Explain how to seek a second chance following a personal mistake.
- Explain the challenges of honest communication.
- Express feelings with words.
- Identify adults on campus and understand their roles.
- Identify supportive adults in various settings (home, school, community).
- Illustrate how connections to school adults support educational endeavors.
- Incorporate feedback from school adults.
- Initiate, sustain and end conversations appropriately and effectively with adults.
- Integrate corrective feedback.
- Interpret adults' verbal social cues.
- Interpret adults' nonverbal social cues.
- List benefits of communicating personal stories, needs/wants, etc.
- Listen with emotional control to constructive feedback from adults.
- Model best voice tone, sound or delivery when talking with an adult.
- Monitor voice tone and volume of others in conversation.
- Name healthy boundaries in relationships with adults.
- Rehearse self-soothing strategies that enable emotional maturity.
- Regulate emotions during social interactions with adults.

- Script a message to request remediation or extra credit from a teacher.
- Seek help or support from adults in various settings (home, school, community).
- Suggest three strategies for building a positive relationship with school adults.

Effective strategies to use or suggest to teachers might include:
- Offer mentoring activities, in which school counselors facilitate large-group time with planned activities for mentors and mentees together; offer students a guided social experience with safe adults.
- Use the 2 X 10 process – adult spends two minutes a day for 10 days engaged in conversation with the student. The conversations focus on getting to know the student rather than anything school related. School counselors may use this strategy or may facilitate the pairing of students in need with adults in the building who are willing/able to build the positive relationships.
- Use dialogue journals, which allow a student and a teacher/school counselor to converse with each other via letter writing. School counselors may be the adult with whom the student is communicating or may facilitate the pairing of students who might need connection with a specific adult in the building who is willing/able to build a positive relationship.
- Provide professional development for faculty/staff on building community within classrooms.
- Conduct book studies with faculty/staff for enhancing their understanding of effective communication with students, current student populations, cultural competence, privilege and oppression, etc.

B-SS 4. Empathy

Empathy is a valuable lifetime skill. It strengthens relationships, encourages acceptance of others and contributes to better mood and happiness. Students who have empathy tend to display:
- Greater class engagement
- Higher academic achievement
- Better communication skills
- More positive relationships
- Fewer behavioral and emotional issues

Empathy has been defined as the cognitive ability to understand how someone might feel and the affective capacity to share those feelings. Others have added compassionate empathy to the definition which moves one to help in some way. Understanding empathy through these three concepts may help guide school counselors as they seek to foster empathy in students.

Cognitive empathy is dependent on recognizing and interpreting body language and facial expressions, incorporating that with what we know of the individual and our own perspectives, to make an educated guess on how that person is feeling. Helping another strengthen their capacity for empathy may start with teaching them to recognize cues.

Affective empathy involves setting aside one's own experiences, judgments and answers to understand the how and why of the feelings observed. It includes listening carefully and patiently and then trying to connect to whatever feelings they are experiencing.

Compassionate empathy is understanding how someone feels and taking appropriate action to help. It may be as straightforward as asking the individual what help they might need. Specific suggestions are offered as possibilities. It is the act of doing something helpful for the individual.

In his book "Working with Emotional Intelligence," Daniel Goleman (2011) identifies five key elements of empathy:

1. Understanding others – reads emotional cues, shows sensitivity, understands others' perspectives
2. Developing others – acts on others' needs, acts with others, gives and receives feedback, helping others develop their full potential, mentors
3. Have a service orientation – puts needs of others first, acts
4. Leveraging diversity – recognizes and celebrates contributions of everyone
5. Political awareness – senses and responds to group emotional undercurrents and power relationships

Foundational Mindsets

The mindsets foundational to this student standard include:

M 1. Belief in development of whole self, including a healthy balance of mental, social/emotional and physical well-being

M 2. Sense of acceptance, respect, support and inclusion for self and others in the school environment

Student Learning Objective Statements

You may choose to copy one of the objectives below, modify to meet your plan more specifically, or create your own. There is also a bank of learning objectives available in the ASCA Student Standards learning objectives database.

This list of learning objectives is not exhaustive nor are the objectives listed in any special order. These are examples of student learning objectives that are linked to this standard. A few of the statements below offer options for refining the focus within the statement. The school counselor should select or define the appropriate focus when incorporating one of those statements.

Consider the context in which this information will be delivered to students as that may affect learning objective selection or creation. The setting can both enhance and limit certain activities and strategies. Knowing if this will be delivered via small-group, classroom or large-group settings may guide the decision. In addition, the primary focus of the work, whether academic, career or social/emotional, aids in the selection/creation process. The primary domain in which the student standard is being addressed may help refine the objective.

Students will:
- Act on identified needs and concerns of others.
- Build a feelings vocabulary commensurate with developmental level.
- Classify responses to a traumatic story as helpful, neutral, unhelpful.
- Convey sensitivity for needs and concerns of others.

- Define the complexities of emotions (types, expressions, intensities, how/when may occur, etc.)
- Define patience and explain its benefits.
- Outline what humans need to live and thrive.
- Demonstrate active listening skills.
- Develop own personal narrative of how they have experienced school/world/life.
- Employ self-soothing strategies in moments of conflict (discomfort, stress, worry, etc.)
- Explain the fluidity of thoughts and emotions, which may vary quickly over a short period of time.
- Express feelings with words.
- Identify active listening processes.
- Identify common problems encountered by students in their age group/grade level (anxiety, emotional dysregulation, worries, fears, relationship concerns, etc.).
- Illustrate how one's own behaviors and words affect others.
- Indicate the connections between thoughts, feelings and behaviors.
- Interpret verbal social cues.
- Interpret nonverbal social cues.
- Investigate the stories, opinions, perspectives and experiences of others.
- Name the steps of effective conflict mediation.
- Paraphrase another's experience accurately.
- Participate in school-sponsored altruistic projects.
- Pause 5-10 seconds before responding to someone's opinion/story/idea/suggestion.
- Recognize and interpret body language and facial expressions.
- Recognize and name feelings in self and others.
- Solve conflicts peacefully.
- Summarize and/or paraphrase perspectives of others.
- Summarize the connections between thoughts and emotions.
- Write responses to a traumatic event.

Effective strategies to use or suggest to teachers might include:
- Ensure all adults in the school model empathy. Consider calling attention to specific moments when empathy and action have occurred.
- Teach what empathy is and why it matters. Highlight examples as they occur.
- Use restorative justice practices and peer mediation.
- Implement an evidence-based social/emotional learning program.
- Design activities to build cultural competence and acceptance of others, and take actions to counter the various "isms" that become evident in the school, community and world.
- Implement regular discussions about emotions to build students' awareness of different emotions, how they might be expressed, what cues suggest those emotions, and help students build a vocabulary bank for naming those emotions. Maintaining an emotion vocabulary board or display reinforces words already discussed and allows for additional words to be added.
- Teach social cues. Students need practice interpreting facial expressions, body language, tone of voice, etc. Collect and display pictures representing clear emotions. Students may also create personal pictures for emotions. These could be added to the emotion vocabulary display.

- Use literature (short stories or novel studies) or media (movie clips or videos) to help students think about emotions and motives of characters.
  - Have students enact a frozen tableau within the story. Each character then unfreezes to explain how they are feeling and thinking and what they might do next.
  - Work in small groups with each group selecting a moment in the story to explore the characters' thoughts, feelings, motives, plans, etc.
  - Talk about "being in someone else's shoes." Ask students to place themselves in a character's mind/circumstance and explain their thoughts, feelings, motivations. Several students may be assigned the same character and begin with an independent reflection. Then, students form groups based on assigned characters, with all members of a group focused on the same character to compare thoughts and insights. Finally, students form groups so that each group has at least one student representative for each character explored in the activity. This discussion focuses on the explanation of each character as well as the interaction of them all.
- Use optical illusions to talk about perspective taking. Show one illusion at a time and have students write what they see. Students then chat with neighbors to discover what others see.
- Conduct discussions allowing students to offer personal opinions and thoughts in small groups. Discussing a favorite book, movie, sport, etc. allows for a variety of opinions to be presented and explained. These brief discussions increase awareness of personal preferences and help students respect/appreciate those differences.
- Role-play social encounters. Provide a brief prompt and allow students time to create and practice their role play. Students demonstrate their play for the class, then respond to questions about what each person in the encounter was thinking and feeling.
- Teach adolescents about the variability of emotions, often experienced intensely in this developmental stage in unpredictable and mercurial moments.
- Provide opportunities for role-play and/or charades for acting out emotions.
- Provide professional development for teachers to conduct morning meetings in classrooms.
- Encourage projects designed to improve some aspect of a class or the school (class gardens, service-learning projects, etc.).
- Conduct class and group instruction on empathy, perspective taking, acceptance of others, etc.
- Discuss current events and ask students to identify how people in the story might be feeling.
- Implement daily morning meetings to give teachers and students a chance to check in on how they are feeling or what they are experiencing. This builds awareness and creates more opportunities for providing support.

B-SS 5. Ethical decision-making and social responsibility

Students need to understand the process required to make good decisions. Typically, the usual steps for deciding can be illustrated in a variety of graphic organizers (tree, flow chart, if/then chart, mind map, etc.). The typical steps included in most models are:

- Determine/define primary problem. This step can be challenging as it may be hard to narrow the problem to an agreed-upon issue.
- Gather any needed information. Decisions should be based on the best available facts, data or knowledge. This step answers the question: What do I need to know?

- Brainstorm various solutions to the problem. When possible, it is best to have a range of options.
- Eliminate solutions that might have serious negative consequences. This step is not always included in various models, but with children and adolescents this may be a critical step. It allows for the removal of those extreme, obviously poor choices that they sometimes include. Adding this step allows for recognition of those possibilities, discussion about consequences and ultimate discard.
- Evaluate remaining options to determine which is best. This step may include identifying pros and cons of each. Selecting the one option with the best chance of success for all is the goal (not necessarily simply the one with the fewest cons).
- Select one solution. Be sure all are aware of the potential outcomes. It may even be possible to combine some of the options.
- Make a plan for executing the identified solution and then do it.
- Review the decision. Identify what worked and what did not. This step will help you make a better decision next time.

Social responsibility is being personally invested in the well-being others, the school, the community and the planet. It can include the production of goods and services in a way that is not harmful to the society or environment. Social responsibility is acting for the benefit of society at large.

Foundational Mindsets
The mindsets foundational to this student standard include:
M 2. Sense of acceptance, respect, support and inclusion for self and others in the school environment
M 4. Self-confidence in ability to succeed
M 5. Belief in using abilities to their fullest to achieve high-quality results and outcomes

Student Learning Objective Statements
You may choose to copy one of the objectives below, modify to meet your plan more specifically, or create your own. There is also a bank of learning objectives available in the ASCA Student Standards learning objectives database.

This list of learning objectives is not exhaustive nor are the objectives listed in any special order. These are examples of student learning objectives that are linked to this standard. A few of the statements below offer options for refining the focus within the statement. The school counselor should select or define the appropriate focus when incorporating one of those statements.

Consider the context in which this information will be delivered to students as that may affect learning objective selection or creation. The setting can both enhance and limit certain activities and strategies. Knowing if this will be delivered via small-group, class-room or large-group settings may guide the decision. In addition, the primary focus of the work, whether academic, career or social/emotional, aids in the selection/creation process. The primary domain in which the student standard is being addressed may help refine the objective.

Students will:

- Analyze prevalent issues occurring in their own community, country and world.
- Ascertain the primary problem from proposed scenarios.
- Brainstorm three to five possible solutions to stated problems.
- Categorize effectiveness and ineffectiveness in own problem-solving methods.
- Categorize positive and negative uses for social media.
- Classify possible solutions as unhealthy/inappropriate, neutral or healthy/appropriate.
- Connect school/class attendance to school success.
- Create a personal standard of ethical conduct.
- Create a rubric for evaluating information resources.
- Critique common rules and values for what is right/wrong or acceptable/unacceptable.
- Debate the benefits and dangers of technology.
- Define social responsibility.
- Delineate steps of an effective decision-making model.
- Describe how they can prevent/stop a rumor from spreading.
- Distinguish multiple perspectives within a given event or circumstance.
- Engage in safe and productive ways to use technology for educational purposes.
- Establish criteria for selecting a solution or course of action from a brainstormed list.
- Explain ethical behavior.
- Formulate ways to contribute to society (volunteering, service-learning, etc.).
- Gather information to make informed decisions.
- Generate a list of resources providing accurate and complete information.
- Give examples of the impact of rumors.
- Identify rumors.
- Illustrate how one's actions affect others.
- Implement a decision-making model.
- List processes and rules for respectful debate.
- Model a reasoned response to conflict.
- Outline an ethical decision-making model.
- Review recent decisions for effectiveness.
- Seek assistance when confronted with dangerous situations or unhealthy behaviors.

Effective strategies to use or suggest to teachers might include:
- Provide instruction on developmentally appropriate decision-making models to students. Provide opportunities to apply the model across subjects, settings and student populations.
- Decision-making models can be applied to problems that occur in:
  - Events or stories found in literature, history, news, etc. Younger children might apply a decision model to a fairy tale, nursery rhyme or simple story; older students might apply the model to more complex stories or events.
  - Peer conflicts – students who seek assistance or are sent for help can fill in a decision-making graphic organizer with each other and/or the school counselor.
  - School or class decisions – use the decision model to plan a class party, field trip or to determine ways to show acquired knowledge.
- Encourage and support local activism by creating or supporting school clubs promoting social responsibility. Link student/school clubs with community organizations promoting school responsibility. First efforts will need to consider:
  - How to choose an issue/project

- What can be accomplished
- How to develop an effective plan
- How to identify and navigate conflicts/barriers
■ Projects/action might include:
  - Organize a program on a specific issue with panel discussions and guest speakers
  - Create a series of PA broadcasts
  - Organize a school action club
  - Prepare school displays to disseminate information
  - Write letters/emails or make phone calls to local, state, national representatives
  - Volunteer to work for an organization or cause

B-SS 6. Effective collaboration and cooperation skills

Collaboration and cooperation involve the interpersonal and cognitive skills necessary to work with others. They are important skills for success in the educational setting, as well as the world of work. They can be viewed as both distinct and overlapping. Collaboration focuses on multiple people working together to create something new based on a shared vision and a common goal. Cooperation is more broadly defined as the exchange of information and resources to support individuals' goals. Whether used as synonyms or seen as distinct, both concepts intersect.

Specific skills are relevant to collaboration and cooperation, including but not limited to:
■ Establishing and maintaining positive relationships
■ Identifying priorities
■ Defining problems (clarity, respect, absence of blame/threats)
■ Listening well (patiently, nonjudgmentally)
■ Communicating effectively (stating ideas, opinions, disagreeing respectfully)
■ Involving everyone
■ Asking good questions
■ Giving and receiving feedback
■ Making relevant contributions
■ Expanding on others' ideas (linking, connecting, broadening, deepening)
■ Sharing information, ideas, suggestions
■ Offering encouragement
■ Checking for agreement, understanding, commitment
■ Resolving conflicts and disputes respectfully and peacefully (fruitful controversy)
■ Compromising (negotiating and building consensus)
■ Taking turns
■ Maintaining focus
■ Sharing credit (acknowledging skills, knowledge, creativity, contributions of others)
■ Supporting group decisions
■ Achieving the task

Foundational Mindsets
The mindsets foundational to this student standard include:
M 3. Sense of acceptance, respect, support and inclusion for self and others in the school environment
M 5. Belief in using abilities to their fullest to achieve high-quality results and outcomes

Student Learning Objective Statements

You may choose to copy one of the objectives below, modify to meet your plan more specifically, or create your own. There is also a bank of learning objectives available in the ASCA Student Standards learning objectives database.

This list of learning objectives is not exhaustive nor are the objectives listed in any special order. These are examples of student learning objectives that are linked to this standard. A few of the statements below offer options for refining the focus within the statement. The school counselor should select or define the appropriate focus when incorporating one of those statements.

Consider the context in which this information will be delivered to students as that may affect learning objective selection or creation. The setting can both enhance and limit certain activities and strategies. Knowing if this will be delivered via small-group, classroom or large-group settings may guide the decision. In addition, the primary focus of the work, whether academic, career or social/emotional, aids in the selection/creation process. The primary domain in which the ASCA Student Standard is being addressed may help refine the objective.

Students will:
- Acknowledge others' skills, knowledge, creativity and contributions.
- Appraise priorities within a problem area or issue.
- Ask clarifying questions.
- Build consensus.
- Collaborate on large projects or endeavors.
- Construct rules for respectful dialogue and debate.
- Contribute to group projects.
- Cooperate with classmates in group endeavors.
- Define problems with clarity and respect.
- Demonstrate how to find solutions to conflicts when working collaboratively with a partner who has a differing opinion.
- Describe individuals in a scenario (e.g., their traits, motivations or feelings) and explain how their actions contribute to the sequence of events.
- Describe the process, purpose and benefits of collaboration and cooperation.
- Determine when and if collaboration and/or cooperation is appropriate.
- Distinguish the language of praise and encouragement.
- Engage in and contribute to collaborative processes/groups.
- Explain problems without blaming or threatening.
- Express own ideas, suggestions and opinions.
- Incorporate constructive feedback.
- Initiate, sustain and end conversations with others.
- Interpret verbal and nonverbal social cues.
- Iterate connections among multiple ideas, opinions and suggestions offered.
- List underlying skills needed to cooperate and/or collaborate.
- Listen effectively.
- Negotiate and compromise in group settings.
- Organize the focus and work of group projects.

- Paraphrase perspectives of others.
- State feedback for ideas, suggestions and opinions.
- State personal opinions, knowledge and/or experiences.
- Summarize and/or paraphrase perspectives of others.
- Support the group decisions.

Effective strategies to use or suggest to teachers might include:
- Provide instruction on the purpose, traits and benefits of collaboration and cooperation.
- Teach the vocabulary and skills of collaboration and cooperation.
- Use cooperative learning experiences in classroom lessons.
- Create "Looks Like, Sounds Like, Feels Like" charts around key concepts and skills of collaboration and cooperation. Examples:

Trait/Skill	Looks Like	Sounds Like	Feels Like
Contributing ideas	Leaning forward Open posture Taking turns Listening	I suggest... We could ... What if we ...	Getting along Positive I get a chance to talk
Checking for understanding	Eye contact Leaning forward Interested expressions Open gestures and posture Everyone involved	Explain that to me, please. Can you show me... How did you get that answer? Give me an example.	Safe A little scary Being thoughtful

B-SS 7. Leadership and teamwork skills to work effectively in diverse teams

Leadership and teamwork are valuable and ubiquitous skills required today. School classes, assignments, tasks and projects incorporate teamwork. Jobs often require teamwork, making it an important career-readiness skill. Leadership is also valued in the workplace, and schools offer many opportunities for practice.

Teamwork depends on all members being committed and engaged while being willing to assume various leadership roles. Making teams work includes setting expectations early, talking about them and maintaining continuous emphasis on those expectations. Members need to fully understand personal roles and responsibilities and feel safe expressing ideas and needs. Associated skills include knowing how to relate and interact with others, knowing how to blend varying ways members function, utilizing each member's strengths, supporting their challenges and creating a well-defined plan for successful completion of the project or task.

Teamwork skills include:
- Active listening
- Questioning
- Logical argument

- Respecting
- Helping
- Sharing
- Participating

Leadership is the act of organizing, motivating and equipping a group toward a common goal or vision. It helps members realize their own potentials. It necessitates being able to inspire others around some idea (generated or created). A leader provides direction for a group, works to ensure needed resources are available and works to maintaining movement toward project or task completion. It is also important to remember the role of leader can rotate among members of the group organically or through specific design.

Leadership skills/traits include:
- Relationship management
- Vision articulation
- Strategic thinking
- Decisive action
- Persuasive communication
- Motivation development
- Leadership development
- Ability to be vulnerable
- Conflict resolution

Team diversity increases the team's creativity, innovation and productivity. Diversity may be represented in a variety of ways: age, nationality, gender, gender identity, sexual orientation, religious background, political preferences, skill level, experience, etc. Steering students toward greater appreciation of those differences requires explicit instruction, courageous conversations and intentional focus. Most teams are diverse in at least one dimension. Teams may also be created to specifically include a greater number of differences between members. It will be important to help students appreciate the benefits of team diversity and to confront the biases, prejudices and assumptions students may hold.

Foundational Mindsets
The mindsets foundational to this student standard include:
M 2. Sense of acceptance, respect, support and inclusion for self and others in the school environment. of belonging in the school environment.
M 4. Self-confidence in ability to succeed
M 6. Positive attitude toward work and learning

Student Learning Objective Statements
You may choose to copy one of the objectives below, modify to meet your plan more specifically, or create your own. There is also a bank of learning objectives available in the ASCA Student Standards learning objectives database.

This list of learning objectives is not exhaustive nor are the objectives listed in any special order. These are examples of student learning objectives that are linked to this standard. A few of the statements below offer options for refining the focus within the statement. The school counselor should select or define the appropriate focus when incorporating one of those statements.

Consider the context in which this information will be delivered to students as that may affect learning objective selection or creation. The setting can both enhance and limit certain activities and strategies. Knowing if this will be delivered via small-group, classroom or large-group settings may guide the decision. In addition, the primary focus of the work, whether academic, career or social/emotional, aids in the selection/creation process. The primary domain in which the student standard is being addressed may help refine the objective.

Students will:
- Articulate a vision for a specific project or task to be completed by a group.
- Characterize various roles with a working group.
- Create a visual map for the completion of a group project, identifying and assigning all roles and responsibilities of group members.
- Create rules for debate.
- Define the underlying skills needed to be an effective leader.
- Define various roles within group work.
- Demonstrate teamwork.
- Describe group stages.
- Determine when to lead and when to follow as a group member.
- Develop strategies to ensure completion of the group task or project.
- Engage in a range of collaborative discussions with diverse partners on how to promote citizenship in school, at home and within the community.
- Establish ground rules for the exchange of ideas and opinions within a task group.
- Establish rules/guidelines for communicating ideas.
- Execute various roles with a group or team effectively.
- Explain the benefits of a team with diverse membership.
- Facilitate involvement of all group members toward task/project completion.
- Formulate persuasive arguments for the purpose or final product of a group.
- Give examples of leadership roles and skills.
- Identify individuals who have made unrecognized, unacknowledged or unpublicized contributions in a specific field (science, writing, art, music, math, literature, etc.).
- Identify personal contributions to a team process.
- Implement conflict resolution techniques/steps within groups.
- List group processes.
- Name personal strengths linked to leadership.
- Name the underlying skills needed to be an effective group member.
- Notice and name contributions of diverse team members.
- Organize group work to ensure contributions of all members.
- Outline a process for reaching consensus within a group.
- Participate in groups/teams in a variety of settings.
- Revise plans and processes as needed based on group membership input.
- Understand the complex constellation of strengths and challenges that comprise heroes, famous individuals, historical figures, etc.

Effective strategies to use or suggest to teachers might include:

- Design/encourage opportunities for student teams to work on projects (courses, grade levels, interest groups, schoolwide).
- Work with students to create "looks like, sounds like, feels like" charts on leadership and teamwork.
- Routinely employ team-building activities for students in class and or group settings. Myriad resources are available for fun, interesting and effective team-building activities. When choosing, be sure to focus on those that require the completion of a specific task in a short amount of time. Examples include:
  - Building a tall tower with toothpicks and marshmallows
  - Creating a raft from popsicle sticks, tape and rubber bands that will float some predetermined item
  - Playing the "human knot" in which a group of students stand in a circle, reach across to grasp right hands with another member who is not beside them, repeat with left hands. Then, attempt to untangle the knot.
  - Inventing and designing something that will make school easier (or any other reason you might identify)
- Intentionally include activities around diversity appreciation in all lessons and activities.
  - Booklists are available online that identify titles of books addressing diversity. Do not limit children's books to children. A good book with a powerful message can be used with any age group. In addition, establish a rubric or criteria for choosing these books. Consider:
    - ▶ Storyline must be interesting
    - ▶ Message must be valid and authentic (best if delivered subtly)
    - ▶ Illustrations should be authentic representations of a variety of people
    - ▶ Readability – can be read aloud easily and within a needed time frame
  - Book studies in which the primary characters are from underrepresented groups
- Advocate for schoolwide adoption of programs and practices reflecting an appreciation of diversity.
- Provide professional development for faculty/staff on how to incorporate leadership and teamwork activities into courses, interest groups, clubs, teams, etc.

B-SS 8. Advocacy skills for self and others and ability to assert self, when necessary

Advocacy is action taken by individuals to solve a problem. It includes active support for an idea or a cause with the intent to influence others' opinions and decisions, thereby generating positive change. Basic tenets of advocacy include the art of persuasion, logical arguments, building relationships, short-term and long-term thinking, persistence and knowledge of the problem's causes and impact as well as the identification of the targeted audience most likely to effect change. Effective advocacy requires all of these.

Advocacy can be categorized as:
- Self-advocacy: action taken by individuals to advance their own interests
- Peer advocacy: action taken by people to safeguard others' rights and interests
- Systems advocacy: action taken that may influence social, political or economic systems producing positive change for a specific group of people
- Legal advocacy: action taken via legal avenues to establish or protect legal rights

Important advocacy skills include:
- Clearly defining the problem
- Identifying appropriate type of advocacy to employ
- Building expertise via education and research
- Developing the right attitude for persistence and assertion
- Following up

Self-advocacy fosters a sense of greater capacity for creating positive change, which leads to an increased sense of hope for managing one's own life and future. That sense of hope and capacity is critical to students' personal motivation and effort. Self-advocacy is the ability to articulate your own needs and to make informed decisions. Effective self-advocacy also fosters an increased sense of responsibility for personal goals, accomplishments and setbacks.

Self-advocacy is an on-going process that necessitates self-monitoring as one evaluates how things are going, makes any needed adjustments and continues with modifications. One might consider these steps in the self-advocacy process:
1. Identify own strengths, challenges and needs.
2. Identify the issue or concern that will be addressed.
3. Identify the person or persons to whom the advocacy will be targeted.
4. Clarify and articulate the specific message to be delivered. Practice saying it effectively.
5. Choose the method that will best convey the message. It may involve direct, individual conversations; a well-written letter or email; a team meeting, etc.
6. Consider and plan for what to do next if the advocacy efforts are effective or if they are not.

Foundational Mindsets
The mindsets which are foundational to this student standard include:
M 1. Belief in development of whole self, including a healthy balance of mental, social/emotional, and physical well-being
M 4. Self-confidence in ability to succeed

Student Learning Objective Statements
You may choose to copy one of the objectives below, modify to meet your plan more specifically, or create your own. There is also a bank of learning objectives available in the ASCA Student Standards learning objectives database.

This list of learning objectives is not exhaustive nor are the objectives listed in any special order. These are examples of student learning objectives that are linked to this standard. A few of the statements below offer options for refining the focus within the statement. The school counselor should select or define the appropriate focus when incorporating one of those statements.

Consider the context in which this information will be delivered to students as that may affect learning objective selection or creation. The setting can both enhance and limit certain activities and strategies. Knowing if this will be delivered via small-group, classroom or large-group settings may guide the decision. In addition, the primary focus of the work, whether academic, career or social/emotional, aids in the selection/creation process. The primary domain in which the student standard is being addressed may help refine the objective.

Students will:
- Build vocabulary for various emotions commensurate with developmental level.
- Clarify a specific issue/concern/problem that is creating barriers or limits for a specific population of students.
- Craft a logical argument on behalf of self/others to address an identified issue/concern/problem.
- Describe the steps for fair arguments.
- Determine a long-term (or short-term) goal and a plan for reaching it.
- Devise a plan for gathering reliable, accurate information around an identified issue/concern/problem.
- Differentiate between being assertive and aggressive.
- Enumerate specific skills associated with persuasion.
- Establish boundaries for courageous conversations.
- Execute goal plans.
- Explain how self-advocacy contributes to one's or someone else's success.
- Explain the role of relationships in advocacy.
- Formulate an assertive statement to advocate for yourself or someone else when necessary.
- Give examples of persistence through barriers/challenges to reaching goals.
- Give examples of personal ideas and contributions to individuals, groups and/or classes.
- Identify individuals who can authorize or generate change around the identified issue/concern/problem.
- Identify others who will support, listen to and help them in advocacy work.
- Illustrate the interplay between personal needs/wants, others' needs/wants and the community's needs/wants.
- Implement a step-by-step approach for responding to teasing and/or bullying behaviors.
- Know when to ask for help.
- List personal strengths and challenges.
- List respectful communication skills and guidelines.
- Locate assistance when confronted with dangerous situations or unhealthy behaviors.
- Map a multilayered advocacy plan around a systemic issue/concern/problem.
- Name standard social rules/guidelines for respectful debate.
- Name ways in which they can use personal strengths to support personal challenges.
- Outline specific impact of the identified issue/concern/problem.
- Recognize personal needs and wants and be able to distinguish between them.
- Script a public service announcement providing information and motivation to act around a specific issue/concern/problem.
- Teach others how to ask for help.

Effective strategies to use or suggest to teachers might include:
- Provide instruction on rules for fair arguments.
  - Establish ground rules
  - Stay calm
  - Use words to convey emotions

- Explain the issue clearly and accurately (specific, no exaggeration, fact-based)
- Maintain focus on current issue only
- Be respectful (language, word choice, no attacks)
- Avoid blame or accusations
- Don't generalizing (always, never)

■ Provide opportunities for students to safely explore and identify their personal strengths and challenges. Classes may brainstorm strengths and challenges students like them might experience. Identify what might be needed for each of the challenges mentioned and how students might advocate for those needs. Focus on how strengths can be used to augment or address challenges.

■ Demonstrate that individuals have a combination of both strengths and challenges that others may not realize. No one is all strengths or all challenges. Students may create face masks on which they write what the world perceives about them on the outward facing side. On the inward facing side of the mask, they identify things about themselves that others may not see or realize. Discuss the benefit of allowing someone to know about a personal challenge and how self-advocacy can build support for needs.

B-SS 9. Social maturity and behaviors appropriate to the situation and environment

Understanding the concepts behind this standard is important. The commonality of the use of terms like maturity and social maturity, and the corresponding use of immature as student descriptors, suggest that everyone is operating from some standard connotation. However, it may reflect more of the individuals' beliefs about what each means rather than actual meaning. Therefore, clarifying each is worth a moment.

Maturity requires the cognitive and social capacities that develop over time and with age and experience. A person who evidences maturity is said to have:
■ Good judgment
■ Sense of responsibility for own thoughts, feelings and behaviors
■ Metacognitive skills (able to track and think about one's own thinking)
■ An understanding of cause and effect
■ The ability to connect current behaviors/actions with future outcomes/consequences

Maturity regulates reasoning, personal responsibility, shared communications, emotional control, openness to new ideas and the ability to find solutions. Two distinct types of maturity are described. Cognitive maturity relates to how one thinks, processes knowledge, grasps abstract concepts, analyzes and learns. Social maturity is how people relate to the society in which they live. Both types of maturity progress over time in successive stages.

Social maturity develops across the lifespan. Infants exist in a world of subjectivity, lacking self-awareness and defined only by needs (hungry, thirsty, tired) to a self that moves toward objectivity, recognition of self as separate from others, needs as manageable, others as more than a source for getting needs met and perspectives as diverse. Eventually, social maturity evolves with the establishment of personal values and ethical codes and realization that there are diverse ways in which others interpret and define their values and ethics. Appreciation of multiple perspectives on the social world and personal standards for living are critical to the process.

The skills associated with social maturity include, but are not limited to:

- Self-awareness
    - Self-regulation or self-control (impulse control, thought stopping, ability to wait)
    - Emotional competence (skills for identifying feelings of self and others, skills for communicating emotions with others, skills for coping with emotions and setbacks)
- Perspective taking
- Empathy
- Relationship skills
- Reflection
- Situational awareness

Foundational Mindsets

The mindsets foundational to this student standard include:

M 1. Belief in development of whole self, including a healthy balance of mental, social/emotional, and physical well-being

M 4. Self-confidence in ability to succeed

Student Learning Objective Statements

You may choose to copy one of the objectives below, modify to meet your plan more specifically, or create your own. There is also a bank of learning objectives available in the ASCA Student Standards learning objectives database.

This list of learning objectives is not exhaustive nor are the objectives listed in any special order. These are examples of student learning objectives that are linked to this standard. A few of the statements below offer options for refining the focus within the statement. The school counselor should select or define the appropriate focus when incorporating one of those statements.

Consider the context in which this information will be delivered to students as that may affect learning objective selection or creation. The setting can both enhance and limit certain activities and strategies. Knowing if this will be delivered via small-group, class-room or large-group settings may guide the decision. In addition, the primary focus of the work, whether academic, career or social/emotional, aids in the selection/creation process. The primary domain in which the student standard is being addressed may help refine the objective.

Students will:

- Analyze the triggers in a scenario that explain the conflict between two or more individuals.
- Clarify personal ideas and perceptions in a discussion.
- Elucidate the connection between current behavior and ultimate outcomes.
- Complete promises and commitments.
- Create a strategy to resolve the conflict between two or more individuals as described in each scenario.
- Create social connections with peers and adults.
- Critique social problems and the varying perspectives associated with each.
- Define responsibility for own actions and behaviors.

- Characterize the complexities of effective communication.
- Determine the meaning of words and phrases that may trigger anger.
- Develop solutions in response to stressful situations or events.
- Distinguish different perspectives around current events and/or issues.
- Examine and reflect on personal thoughts, feelings and actions following challenging experiences or setbacks.
- Explain social justice.
- Explain various "isms" (racism, genderism, classism, ableism, etc.).
- Give personal examples of lessons learned from a personal setback.
- Identify personal strengths and challenges.
- Implement a variety of coping strategies for challenging emotions, encounters, experiences, conditions and circumstances.
- Incorporate self-soothing strategies to maintain personal control when experiencing strong emotions and/or setbacks.
- Interpret cues to the emotions of others.
- Manage strong emotions, expressing those feelings without negative consequences.
- Name adults who will support students.
- Publicize contributions made by a diverse set of peers to the school community.
- Recognize and regulate feelings during times of academic and personal stress (mindfulness techniques, such as deep breathing, stretching, reading, collaborative discussions and self-assessment).
- Recognize feelings of others during challenging experiences or encounters.
- Restate key ideas expressed in a discussion.
- Specify the demands of varied situations and environments.
- State personal needs/wants.
- Structure a personal strengths and challenges table.
- Summarize concepts of privilege and oppression.
- Summarize personal feelings during challenging experiences or encounters.
- Use age-appropriate vocabulary for naming emotions.

Effective strategies to use or suggest to teachers might include:

- Teach empathy and perspective taking.
- Teach basic manners. These social standards not only improve students' relationships with others, but they are also a career-readiness skill. Move beyond the mannerly words to include appropriate greetings, personal space, behaviors in different settings, interpreting tone, etc.
- Teach skills of emotional competence (ability to recognize, interpret and respond to emotions in self and others).
- Incorporate games and nondirected play activities into learning experiences. This facilitates ability to wait, take turns, share, work as a team, etc.
- Discuss significant experiences with students. Ask how they feel. Help them make sense of the emotions.
- Use stories to explore social maturity concepts. Develop specific questions to encourage students to understand the situations, challenges and responses of characters in the stories.
  - Read fiction to students. Stories are powerful tools for conveying experiences, emotions, needs, goals, actions. Choose stories that focus on characters who are

original and diverse, who encounter some difficulty and who work to overcome or manage the challenge. Story characters are most relevant when they match the targeted students in some way (similar age, demographic, challenge, etc.). Students may also learn through stories that feature superheroes.

- Use nonfiction literature with students. Focus on real-life individuals who worked for some societal good, including both those who are well-known, by identity and accomplishment, as well as those less famous.

■ Write social stories with students who may be struggling with specific social encounters.

■ Encourage opportunities for students to be involved in team sports and other extracurricular activities.

B-SS 10. Cultural awareness, sensitivity and responsiveness

Culture is complex and multifaceted. Components include thoughts, communication, language, beliefs, customs, rituals, courtesies, roles, religion, values, behaviors and guidelines for interactions and relationships. It is always changing.

Cultural Awareness

Cultural awareness is the identification of the nuances of one's own and other cultures. It has been defined as the first and foundational component of cultural competence, as defined by the National Center for Cultural Competence (n.d.). It includes being mindful, observant and conscious of both similarities and differences between cultural groups. Cultural awareness also includes acknowledgement of one's own cultural influences as well as organizational culture on values, beliefs, judgments, perceptions, practices, biases and policy.

Working through a lens of cultural awareness involves raising awareness of culture's influence and impact on how we act and function in the world. It requires one to be self-aware and to respect the cultures of others. That awareness helps us understand and interact with others.

Cultural Sensitivity

Cultural sensitivity is grounded in an understanding of needs and feelings within one's own culture and the cultures of others. It involves being aware that cultural differences and similarities exist without assigning value, as well as understanding that one way of living is not superior to another. All are valid and deserve respect. This sensitivity moves beyond understanding or acknowledging distinctions to include skills enhancing interpersonal interactions, building collegial relationships, responding appropriately and supporting those of differing backgrounds. Cultural sensitivity has been called a transformative process that acknowledges interdependence.

Cultural Responsiveness

The Early Childhood Learning & Knowledge Center, a subset of the U.S. Department of Health & Human Services, defines cultural responsiveness as a strengths-based approach to teaching and caregiving, grounded in respect and appreciation for how culture operates on learning and development. One who is culturally responsive seeks to know the strengths, abilities, experiences and interests of students. There is a focus on building on those strengths, abilities, experiences and interests while incorporating individuals' cultures into the classroom (Head Start, Early Childhood Learning & Knowledge Center, n.d.).

The California Department of Developmental Services (1997) offers tips for developing cultural responsiveness.
1. Become aware of your own cultural background.
2. Believe that cultural beliefs are not right or wrong. Each is correct in the culture in which it occurs.
3. Make it personal. Establish contact in person or via a phone call.
4. Learn about the people you serve. Seek out community organizations to beginning building and maintaining cultural networks.
5. Educate the community's culturally different leaders about issues, services and rights. Attend and speak at community events. Write articles for culturally focused publications.
6. Use vocabulary of greetings and key phrases in the primary language. It shows a willingness to enter their world.
7. Educate yourself about the cultural beliefs of the people you serve.
8. Use a translator when you are not proficient in someone's preferred language.
9. Try to discover commonalities of experiences. Consider hobbies, styles of cooking, parenting, life experiences. As you find and explore these, the bond strengthens.

Foundational Mindsets
The mindsets foundational to this student standard include:

M1: Belief in development of whole self, including a healthy balance of mental, social/emotional and physical well-being

M2: Sense of acceptance, respect, support and inclusion for self and others in the school environment. of belonging in the school environment

Student Competency/Learning Objective Statements
You may choose to copy one of the objectives below, modify to meet your plan more specifically, or create your own. There is also a bank of learning objectives available in the ASCA Student Standards learning objectives database.

This list of learning objectives is not exhaustive nor are the objectives listed in any special order. These are examples of student learning objectives that are linked to this standard. A few of the statements below offer options for refining the focus within the statement. The school counselor should select or define the appropriate focus when incorporating one of those statements.

Consider the context in which this information will be delivered to students as that may affect learning objective selection or creation. The setting can both enhance and limit certain activities and strategies. Knowing if this will be delivered via small-group, classroom or large-group settings may guide the decision. In addition, the primary focus of the work, whether academic, career or social/emotional, aids in the selection/creation process. The primary domain in which the student standard is being addressed may help refine the objective.

Students will:
- Identify personal cultural beliefs, values and traditions.
- Define various roles within their own cultural backgrounds.
- Name three–five distinctions between their own cultural influences from those of classmates (or teachers).
- Name three–five similarities between their own cultural influences and those of classmates (or teachers).
- Delineate the student body's prevailing cultural beliefs, values and traditions.
- List the various cultures within the school.
- Cite cultural influences on the school's traditions and practices among and with students.
- Cite conflicting cultural influences in the building.
- Describe the impact of conflicting cultural influences in the building.
- Identify barriers and challenges to addressing issues/concerns/problems related to diverse cultural influences.
- Design a plan for illuminating specific cultural issues/concerns/problems in the school.
- Design a plan for planned emphasis on and recognition of each and all cultures in the school.
- Examine common practices in the school that inhibit/limit appreciation for all cultures.
- Explain how the varying cultures in the school enhance the educational experience.
- Evaluate the visuals in and around the school for inclusiveness.
- Clarify ways students may support each other when faced with cultural conflicts.
- Acknowledge the varied lived experiences of students from all cultures.
- Identify the intersections of the cultures co-existing in the school.
- Identify specific strengths and assets of each culture in the school.
- Script public service announcements that facilitate respect and appreciation for how cultural influences operate in the school.

Effective strategies to use or suggest to teachers might include:
- Conduct a building walk-through with a group of students to evaluate the visual displays for inclusivity.
- Identify, post and practice common greetings and phrases of the cultures within the school. Consider emphasizing the use of specific terms each month or week.
- Identify overlapping beliefs and create displays illustrating those overlaps. For example, most cultures have a version of the "golden rule." All can be included in a single display.
- Post a large world map at the entrance of the school. Highlight geographic locations that are the origins for families within the school.
- Schedule specific culture events in which multiple cultures provide a booth or display relevant to their own culture.
- Schedule field trips to nearby locations associated with specific cultures.
- Include cultural emphasis in content areas. For example, art classes may focus on specific types of art associated with specific cultures (worry beads or painted vases/Greek, tissue-paper flowers/Mexican, mosaic sundials or hieroglyphics/Egyptian, cherry blossoms or origami/Asian, rug design/Navajo, etc.). Music, geography, history and literature all offer opportunities for cultural exploration.
- Use students' writings to create classroom books that reveal experiences and traditions of students' cultural backgrounds.

Kristin Burnham (2020), of Northeastern University Graduate Programs, identifies five culturally responsive teaching strategies.

1. Activate students' prior knowledge. Class discussions provide opportunities for students to discuss their own experiences. This helps link current learning to their own lived worlds.
2. Make learning contextual. Connect lessons from curricula to the communities of students, increasing context and relevance.
3. Encourage students to leverage their cultural capital. Incorporate books, stories, experiences of those who reflect the various cultures within the classroom, ensuring that all students have their own cultures and lives reflected in the lessons and activities in the classroom.
4. Reconsider your classroom setup. Pay attention to your classroom visuals to ensure all cultures and communities are represented. Ensure bulletin boards, posters, displays are inclusive. Note the books available in your classroom library, checking that various cultures are respectfully and authentically present
5. Build relationships. Feeling valued, respected and seen as their authentic selves within the classroom is essential for students to want to learn. Those who work to intentionally build community in the classroom and among students enhance learning.

Western Governors University (2021) identifies benefits of culturally responsive teaching.

1. Raises children's expectations of the real world.
2. Helps schools better meet their students' needs.
3. Builds cultural awareness in the classroom and beyond.
4. Helps students feel empowered.
5. Creates a more level educational experience.
6. Facilitates teachers letting go of their biases.
7. Fosters equity in the classroom.
8. Encourages student engagement.
9. Honors unique identifies.

CHAPTER 6

Writing Student Learning Objectives

Learning objectives specify student knowledge and skills targeted through instruction. They succinctly describe what a student will know or be able to do because of that instruction. Well-written learning objectives serve as a guide to what needs to be taught to students. They also provide the basis for assessing students' learning because of that instruction. The learning objective is easily converted to the pre-/post-assessment tool.

Learning objectives follow the same format.
Begin with "Students" as the subject of the sentence.
Follow "Students" with a verb indicating specific, measurable and observable behaviors.
Conclude the statement with a description of the specific knowledge or skill.

Students will _____   _____.
　　　　　　　　　　　action verb　　　　 description of knowledge or skill students will acquire

A Process for Writing Learning Objectives

1. Begin by reflecting on what you hope to accomplish through your instruction.
   a. What specific knowledge and skills are associated with the specific ASCA Student Standard identified as important to students' growth?
   b. What do students need to know to be able to improve their academic performance, college/career readiness, relationships with others and/or social/emotional health?
   c. What do you want students to be able to do as a direct result of the school counselor/ student interaction?

2. Think in terms of knowledge, attitudes and skills. Doing so will help you identify the kind of change you want to see in students.
   a. Knowledge – increasing what students know. These statements specify what you want student to know following the school counselor/student interaction. What new knowledge will be gained?
   b. Attitude – dealing with feelings, beliefs and attitudes. These statements are hard to write and assess. It may help you understand what might need to change for a student as you craft your interventions.

c. Skills – changing, improving or adding to the tasks a student can perform. These statements specify what students will be able to do following the school counselor/ student interaction. What new skills will be gained?

3. Brainstorm, in writing, a list of knowledge and skills based on the thoughts generated by the first two exercises. At this stage, do not stop to consider verb choices or try to create the perfect statement. Simply record your initial thoughts and ideas. Wordsmithing will occur later.

4. Review and hone the brainstormed list.
   a. Check for statements that are about participating in a specific activity or learning experience. For example, "Students will participate in a study skills group" is about the learning activity rather than the student outcome.
      ■ Identify the statements focused on an activity or learning experience.
      ■ Rewrite those statements to focus on the student outcome – what will change because of the activity/experience?
      ■ Eliminate those that cannot be rewritten.
   b. Highlight those that are not knowledge or skills. This includes all statements that focus on values, beliefs, opinions, traits or the way a student feels.
      ■ If possible, rewrite those that can be changed into a specific knowledge or skill students will acquire. For example, "Students will believe = the teacher likes him/ her/them" could be rewritten as "Students will name teachers who will support academic needs."
      ■ Eliminate those that cannot be rewritten to specify knowledge or skill.
   c. Remove all qualitative adjectives from each statement.
      ■ Qualitative adjectives are abstract and are subject to opinions, beliefs and perceptions. They require judgment rather than measuring. Most have three forms: positive, comparative, superlative. All denote a level of quality.
      ■ Qualitative words lessen the clarity of the statement and can make it hard to measure. In addition, they are unnecessary. For example, a learning objective might state, "Students will effectively advocate for academic support." Adding the word "effectively" would necessitate a rubric that defines what "effectively" means and complicates measurement.
      ■ Additionally, the word is not needed as it seems implied that the advocacy skills being taught to students are only those that have the best chance of working. We would not teach ineffective advocacy strategies. Removing the qualitative word results in a statement that can be answer easily – yes, they can or, no, they cannot.
      ■ A sample of qualitative adjectives is provided.

Positive	Comparative	Superlative
Good	Better	Best
Nice	Nicer	Nicest
Happy	Happier	Happiest
Effective	Very Effective	Most Effective
Interesting	Very Interesting	Most Interesting
Honest	More Honest	Most Honest

5. Review the verbs in each learning objective. It is common to use the same words repeatedly. Do not be concerned, as a focus on selecting verbs will stall the brainstorming process. This step provides the opportunity to improve those words.
   a. Consider using the computer's thesaurus to identify other possible verbs. This step can be helpful as it may clarify the intent of the statement. Did the statement mean understand, define, explain or critique? Would you want students to learn or demonstrate? For this step, you may continue to discover that you tend toward using the same words repeatedly.
   b. Use a thesaurus or the Bloom's Taxonomy chart to expand your verbs. It is at this point you will begin to differentiate the level of knowledge or skill you want students to demonstrate. This step is best accomplished after letting your statements rest for a day or two. Return to them when you are no longer influenced by what you think you wrote.
   c. Using words from the Bloom's chart is not required. This suggestion is made simply to help school counselors write clearer learning objectives.
   d. Consider the level of learning evidenced by each statement. Do not work to have objectives applied solely to any one level. It is not helpful to have all statements at either the highest or lowest level. It is best to have a few statements for each of the Bloom's Taxonomy.
   e. Make note of passive voice. This often appears as "will be able to" for the beginning of the statement. To move to active voice, simply strike "be able to." Consider this example: Students will be able to write a clear goal statement including all SMART components. Instead, strike out the "will be able to" to become: Students will write a clear goal statement including all SMART components.

6. Select the most relevant learning objectives (two-five) to use for the specific group of students and the targeted ASCA Student Standard. This step increases the intentionality of lesson plans, learning strategies and specific activities for the planned intervention.

Keep the list of learning objectives you have created for the specific ASCA Student Standard, both those objectives you will use for the planned intervention and those objectives you have determined not to use for this event. Maintaining this personal bank of learning objectives increases efficiency, as they may be useful for another group at another time.

What to Avoid in Learning Objectives
Learning objectives not stated in terms of the student: Writing the objective as something the school counselor will do is a common mistake. The ASCA National Model templates were designed specifically to reduce this error, and all templates that include learning objectives designate that each objective begins with "Students will..." The following templates include learning objectives: annual student outcome goal plan, lesson plans.

Learning objectives that can't be observed or measured: Steps 3, 4, 5 and 6 of the process for writing learning objectives can help you avoid this mistake. Measurement of the objective can be achieved in a variety of ways. You can use your pre-/post assessment to allow for student self-reports on Likert scales regarding their own perception of attainment. In addition, verbal responses, exit slips, completed tasks, card sorts and role-plays represent other ways in which to determine whether students learned.

Learning objectives that are general in scope: Objectives guide both instruction and assessment. Therefore, they should clearly define and limit the exact knowledge and skills relevant to the planned interaction. For example, you may want students to gain knowledge of study skills. The learning objective is best when it defines the study skills to be learned (mnemonic devices, note-taking, task prioritization, creation of study aids for tests).

Learning objectives that are rambling or lengthy: The more words you add, the greater the risk of complicating the statement. Keep the language of the objective focused on what you plan to teach and measure. It improves your teaching and assessment.

Learning objectives unrelated to the specific ASCA Student Standard: The purpose of the learning objectives is to operationalize the selected ASCA Student Standard. Think of what students would be able to do if they mastered the stated standard. What would they know? The objectives clarify the precise knowledge and skills an individual would possess if that standard were attained. Well-stated objectives direct the instruction needed and development of pre-/post-assessments.

Learning objectives unrelated to students' needs: Learning objectives are specific to the group of students who will participate in the school counselor/student interaction. Different groups of students may work toward the same ASCA Student Standard, and it is perfectly appropriate to write a different learning objective for each group of students based on their specific needs.

For example, instruction is being delivered to all classes in a grade level based on B-SMS 2. (Self-discipline and self-control). One group of students may have a teacher who is new to the school and is still navigating new procedures and expectations. The teacher's frustration is leading to frequent changes in school assignments and how to complete them. Students in this class might need to focus on the following learning objectives:
- Students will employ self-calming strategies.
- Students will interpret facial/body/verbal cues of others.

Another class of students in the same grade level may include several students who tend to be louder or more impulsive, as well as some who have a history of not getting along. The interactions of students in the class could contribute to an increased number of disruptions. Those students might need to focus on these objectives:
- Students will explain the reasons for school rules.
- Students will describe how effort and behavior affect outcomes.

Both classes of students will receive instruction on the same standard, but the lessons will be somewhat different to reflect the needs of each group.

Learning Objectives Do's	Learning Objectives Don'ts
■ Make sure there is one measurable verb in each statement ■ Describe what students will know or be able to do ■ Include measurable and/or observable terms describing the knowledge or skill to be acquired by students ■ Be clear and concise about what students will learn ■ Limit your words ■ Write statements directly linked to one student standard ■ Use Bloom's Taxonomy list of words to find the best verbs ■ Use the learning objectives to focus the content of instruction ■ Base pre-/post-test assessments on the stated learning objectives	■ Include multiple verbs in the statement (define and apply, for example): multiple verbs complicate how to determine mastery ■ Write about something the school counselor will know or do ■ Focus on what students will think, believe or feel ■ Focus on global concepts or copious content ■ Include vague words (some, effective, many, best) ■ Include qualitative adjectives ■ Include extra information about a specific activity or strategy that might be used ■ Write statements not connected to the student standard ■ Forget to include a verb ■ Create statements that are only about repeating facts or steps

A Word about Bloom's Taxonomy

The taxonomy was proposed in 1958 by Benjamin Bloom, an educational psychologist at the University of Chicago, along with several colleagues, Max Englehart, Edward Furst, Walter Hill and David Krathwohl, and focused on the cognitive domain. These individuals were trying to define the functions of thought or learning. The taxonomy is hierarchical and specifies levels of learning. Each level is dependent on the knowledge and skills gained in previous levels. Put simply, it is a classification of different objectives and skills desired for students. It has been described as an ordering of cognitive skills and has served as foundational for teacher instruction on creating learning objectives.

In 2001, the taxonomy was revised, primarily by Lorin Anderson and David Krathwohl and an invited group of educational psychologists. Anderson was a student of Bloom's, and Krathwohl was one of Bloom's partners when the taxonomy was created. The revision focused on the interaction between the taxonomy and the different types of knowledge (Wilson, 2020).

The 1956 version of the taxonomy focused on three levels of knowledge:
1. Factual knowledge: knowledge that is basic to specific disciplines, including facts, terminology and details
2. Conceptual knowledge: knowledge of classifications, principles, generalizations, theories, models or structures related to specific disciplines
3. Procedural knowledge: knowledge that helps one do something specific to a discipline, subject or area of study

The 2002 revision added the category of metacognition.
4. Metacognition – knowledge of one's own cognition and cognitive processes.

Bloom's Taxonomy

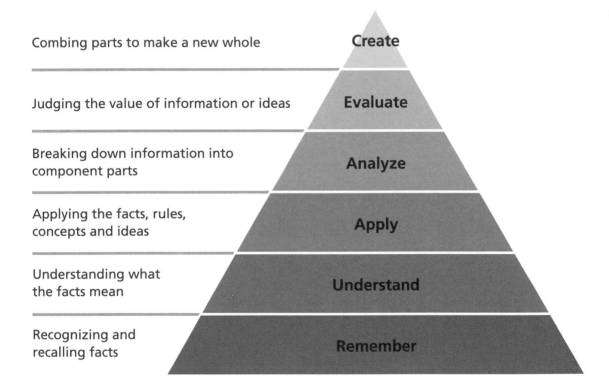

Source: Shabatura, 2013

Examples of Verbs in Bloom's Taxonomy
This list is not an exhaustive and includes those verbs commonly found in charts associated with the taxonomy. You may also discover that words may appear in different columns/categories as you review the many lists available online. Many of the words are synonyms, and it can be challenging to identify the specific differences among them. This list is simply a sampling and is to be used as a guide rather than a fixed and perfect listing.

Remembering	Understanding	Applying	Analyzing	Evaluating	Creating
Define	Annotate	Apply	Analyze	Assess	Argue
Describe	Classify	Calculate	Appraise	Compare	Arrange
Choose	Compile	Compose	Attribute	Critique	Assemble
Define	Conclude	Construct	Categorize	Decide	Brainstorm
Identify	Explain	Demonstrate	Correlate	Debate	Build
Label	Give examples	Determine	Compare	Defend	Compose
List	Illustrate	Develop	Contrast	Detect	Conceive
Match	Indicate	Dramatize	Determine	Determine	conceptualize
Name	Infer	Edit	Differentiate	Establish	Construct
Order	Interpret	Generalize	Discriminate	Evaluate	Create
Recall	Paraphrase	Implement	Distinguish	Judge	Design
Recognize	Report	Locate	Infer	Measure	Diagnose
Select	Summarize	Perform	Integrate	Persuade	Envision
State	Translate	Predict	Manage	Plan	Formulate
		Present	Organize	Prioritize	Hypothesize
		Schedule		Rate	Invent
		Solve		Synthesize	Predict
		Teach		Verify	Publish
		Use			Produce
					Revise
					Strategize
					Write

References

American Psychological Association. (n.d.) Coping. In *APA dictionary of psychology*. Retrieved April 4, 2022, from https://dictionary.apa.org/coping

Bandura, A. (1977). Self-efficacy: Toward a unifying theory of behavioral change. *Psychological Review, 84*(2), 191–215 https://doi.org/10.1037/0033-295X.84.2.191

Bredehoft, D. J. (2019). Delayed gratification in an age of overindulgence. *Psychology Today*. https://www.psychologytoday.com/us/blog/the-age-overindulgence/201910/delayed-gratification-in-age-overindulgence

Burnham, K. (2020.). *5 culturally responsive teaching strategies*. Northeastern University Graduate Programs. https://www.northeastern.edu/graduate/blog/culturally-responsive-teaching-strategies/

Delong, M., & Winter, D. (2002) *Learning to teach and teaching to learn mathematics: Resources for professional development*. Mathematical Association of America.

Department of Developmental Services. (1997). How to be culturally responsive. https://www.dds.ca.gov/wp-content/uploads/2019/03/Publications_CulturallyResponsive_20190318.pdf

Duckworth, A. L., & Seligman, M. E. P. (2005). Self-discipline outdoes IQ in predicting academic performance of adolescents. *Psychological Science, 16*, 939–944 https://doi.org/10.1111/j.1467-9280.2005.01641.x

Elias, M. J. (2019, November 14). A framework for student goal-setting. *Edutopia*. https://www.edutopia.org/article/framework-student-goal-setting

Farrington, C., Johnson, D. W., Allensworth, E., Nagaoka, J., Roderick, M., Beechum, N. W., & Keyes, T. S. (2012, June). *Teaching adolescents to become learners*. University of Chicago Consortium on School Research. https://consortium.uchicago.edu/publications/teaching-adolescents-become-learners-role-noncognitive-factors-shaping-school

Ferlazzo, L. (2015, March 25). Strategies for helping students motivate themselves. *Edutopia*. https://www.edutopia.org/blog/strategies-helping-students-motivate-themselves-larry-ferlazzo

Goleman, D. (2011). *Working with emotional intelligence*. Bantam.

Gonzalez, J. (2016, February 20). 5 questions to ask yourself about your unmotivated students. *Cult of Pedagogy*. https://www.cultofpedagogy.com/student-motivation/

Greater Good in Education. (n.d.) *Positive teacher-student relationships*. https://ggie.berkeley.edu/school-relationships/positive-teacher-student-relationships/#tab__2

Head Start, Early Childhood Learning & Knowledge Center. (n.d.) *Cultural responsiveness*. U.S. Department of Health & Human Services. https://eclkc.ohs.acf.hhs.gov/curriculum/consumer-report/criteria/cultural-responsiveness

Johns Hopkins University Student Assistance Program. (n.d.). School-life balance. https://jhsap.org/self_help_resources/school-life_balance/

Kohn, A. (2018, October 28). Rewards are still bad news (25 years later). *New York Times*. https://www.alfiekohn.org/article/rewards-25-years-later/

National Center for Cultural Competence. (n.d.) *Cultural awareness*. Georgetown University. https://nccc.georgetown.edu/curricula/awareness/index.html

Pickhardt, C. E. (2016, September 19). Adolescence and four skills of self-discipline. *Psychology Today*. https://www.psychologytoday.com/us/blog/surviving-your-childs-adolescence/201609/adolescence-and-four-skills-self-discipline

Pink, D. H. (2011). *Drive: The surprising truth about what motivates us*. Penguin.

Price-Mitchell, M. (2018, March 14). Goal-setting is linked to higher achievement. *Psychology Today*. https://www.psychologytoday.com/us/blog/the-moment-youth/201803/goal-setting-is-linked-higher-achievement

Psychology Today. (n.d.-a). *Creativity*. https://www.psychologytoday.com/us/basics/creativity

Psychology Today. (n.d.-b). *Self-control*. https://www.psychologytoday.com/us/basics/self-control

Scharff, C. (2016, September 16). Understanding and choosing better coping skills. *Psychology Today*. https://www.psychologytoday.com/us/blog/ending-addiction-good/201609/understanding-and-choosing-better-coping-skills

Shabatura, J. (2013, September 27). *Using Bloom's Taxonomy to write effective learning objectives*. University of Arkansas. https://tips.uark.edu/using-blooms-taxonomy/

Shafer, L. (2019, July 17). How attendance awards backfire. *Usable Knowledge, Harvard Graduate School of Education*. https://www.gse.harvard.edu/news/uk/19/07/limits-perfect-attendance-awards

Travers, C., Morisano, D., & Locke, E. A. (2015). Self-reflection, growth goals, and academic outcomes: A qualitative study. *British Journal of Educational Psychology, 85*(2), 224–241. https://doi.org/10.1111/bjep.12059

Trilling, B., & Fadel, C. (2012). *21st Century skills: Learning for life in our times.* Jossey-Bass.

U.S. Bureau of Labor Statistics. (2019, October). Projections overview and highlights, 2018–28, *Monthly Labor Review*. https://www.bls.gov/opub/mlr/2019/article/projections-overview-and-highlights-2018-28.htm

Western Governors University. (2021, November 15). *What is culturally responsive teaching?* https://www.wgu.edu/blog/what-is-culturally-responsive-teaching2111.html

Wilcox, L. (2018, June 4). *Top 5 strategies for motivating students.* National Board for Professional Teaching Standards. https://www.nbpts.org/blog/top-5-strategies-for-motivating-students/

Wilson, L. O. (2020). *Bloom's taxonomy revised.* https://thesecondprinciple.com/essential-teaching-skills/blooms-taxonomy-revised/